"I Always Knew You Weren't Really God"

and Other Tales of an Ordinary Rabbinate

by Rabbi Larry Mahrer

Dem Bones Publishing

Cover and Book design by Scott Mahrer

Printed in the United States of America

First Printing, 2019

ISBN 978-0-578-53250-9

Dem Bones Publishing
Egg Harbor Township, New Jersey 08234

To Debi, Jeff, and Scott
who helped me stay sane
while all these silly events
were happening around me

and to

all the congregants and colleagues,
some mentioned and some not,
who were the characters
in these stories,
who gave me a laugh
or a tear
and who added spice and leavening
to my life.

Table of Contents

Introduction — *Scott Mahrer*

Foreword — *Rabbi Ron Klotz*

Preface   *1*

Shabbat on Thursday? and Other Pre-Rabbinic Stories   *5*

We Were Teenage Rabbis   *17*

We Were Rabbis for Teenagers   *27*

I Also Know I Am Not Isaac Mayer Wise   *43*

A Shabbat Walk and Other Ways of Finding God   *52*

Taking Advantage: Good and Bad   *65*

Sermons and other Sentient Sayings   *76*

Doing Justice: Social Action   *101*

The JCS Made Me A Star   *132*

Significant Moments: Good, Sad, Even Funny   *145*

Miscellaneous Mishugas   *167*

Memorable Moments in an Ordinary Rabbinate   *175*

The Perfect Rabbi   *198*

"I Always Knew You Weren't Really God"   *206*

The End of the Line   *209*

Epilogue   *213*

Afterword   *217*

Glossary   *219*

Introduction

"Whatever you do, don't call him 'Sir.' You can call him 'Rabbi Larry' or 'Rabbi Mahrer.' Just don't use 'Sir.' He has a *thing* about people calling him Sir." That has been my pre-introductory instruction to anyone I have ever brought to meet my father. I never truly understood his issue about that word, and thus really didn't understand his choice to move to South Carolina in 1984. My first response was, "Someone is definitely going to have to get over his thing about being called 'Sir.' They do that a *lot* in South Carolina." I'm sure that I riffed on that theme a bit more at his expense. Ten years later, he moved even further south to Dothan, Alabama.

As a child, I always felt like people borrowed my father without permission. It seemed that he was away from the home quite a bit. His job was certainly not the nine-to-five sort that other dads appeared to hold. I could not understand why there were so many meetings, functions, and visits that he had to attend. Other people required his attention often. Working with the manuscript for this book, I discovered that he felt similarly about his parents and their involvement with the Jewish community. Reading through these pages, I learned a bit about my father, especially from my youngest years. The adult me understands the larger picture that the child me did not.

My father did not always practice what he preached. Whenever he was asked about the proper age to start bringing a child to the regular, adult Friday night *Shabbat* services, he would typically answer, "Nine or ten." That was just not the case for his own kids. While I did not attend every week, I was substantially younger than his suggested age range when I first attended.

The hardest part of the evening to sit through as a child was the sermon. From a child's point of view, nothing happens during that 20 or more minutes. No pages to turn, no one is moving. Just Dad talking. A lot. The synagogue building was new and full of technical marvels, one of which was the speaker system throughout the building. You could hear what was happening in the sanctuary everywhere. This included the kitchen off the Social Hall, where my friend Dan, the custodian, could be found during the sermon. I quickly learned that I could "go to the restroom" as the sermon started and return to my seat once it ended, having spent the time visiting with Dan. That pattern existed for quite some time before my mother realized my consistency.

My father's sermon routine remained the same throughout his rabbinate. As he approached the lectern to give his sermon, he would remove his watch and place it on the upper-left corner of the lectern to remain aware of the time. Once finished, the watch would go back on his wrist, and he would walk back to his seat and sit down. It was during that short walk back to his seat that the organist would begin a brief musical segue that would be followed by an officer of the congregation reading some announcements.

The night arrived when my mother forced me to remain in my seat during the sermon. My father finished and during that very brief, very quiet moment before the music started, I proclaimed in what used to be described as my *outside voice* before being diagnosed as partially deaf, "Jesus Christ, I could have said that in half the time!" It has been said that my voice echoed throughout the room. My father was, by now, seated next to the temple president, who apparently leaned over and said, "The kid may have a point." I'm pretty sure I was not at services held the next week.

Over the years I would point out to my father when he had recycled a sermon. It makes sense why he would recycle a sermon or two as my father served several synagogues and new audiences over his career. The core ideas and lessons would be the same, but the details would be updated to reflect the times or the different location. He steadfastly would deny the said recycling, refusing to admit to it. It's nice to see that he references *a couple* of sermons that he repeated over the years in this book. Small, baby steps indeed.

One sermon stands out to me for a few reasons. It was potentially his most controversial, and it attracted a larger than normal crowd for that particular service. It also, to my knowledge, was the only one that he never finished.

In 1977, we lived in Wausau, Wisconsin. A group of Nazis had applied for a permit to march in Skokie, Illinois, a predominantly Jewish suburb of Chicago. In an effort to prevent the march, the Skokie City Council passed several ordinances that rendered a demonstration by the Nazis virtually impossible. The Nazis filed a First Amendment court case in opposition, and the American Civil Liberties Union (ACLU) represented the group. Adding to the debate was the fact that the ACLU attorney representing their interests in court was Jewish.

During all of this, my father planned a sermon that attempted to objectively talk about how a Jewish ACLU lawyer could possibly represent such a despicable group in court. He started discussing how this man must have weighed his Jewishness against his firm belief in the concept of the Freedom of Speech. Clearly not a painless decision for the lawyer, and not an easy subject of discussion in a synagogue. Adding to the complexity was the fact that the congregation was home to a few Holocaust survivors.

My father has always welcomed his congregation to speak out during a sermon, something I am sure would raise a few eyebrows among some of his colleagues. Understandably, the chosen topic fostered much discussion. As my father attempted to try to stand in the shoes of the Jewish ACLU attorney, the members of the congregation interrupted. They couldn't get past the fact that he was a Jewish lawyer. Being told that the ACLU used a round-robin method of determining who would try cases, that it was simply his turn, didn't help. After 20 minutes of his attempting to present his planned sermon, my father simply stopped, put his watch back on, and realized this was one issue too large for a typical sermon. The discussion continued during the *Oneg Shabbat* afterwards, but never did reach any sort of conclusion.

My father has spoken of this particular sermon as a success. Even with the fact that he was prevented from finishing, the congregation was fully engaged. They were active participants, which I believe pleased my father to no end.

Baby naming ceremonies in the synagogue are a joyous part of life. My father would call the parents up to the *bimah* with their infant. They would stand facing the Ark, with my father facing them. Often, the baby would start crying while being brought up, probably due to being jostled when their parents stood up from their seats. My father would begin reading from the *siddur* (Jewish prayer book), and every crying baby would cease making noise, without exception. The whispers would start, every time, "Did you hear that? The Rabbi just *started* talking and the baby stopped crying!" What the congregation could not see is that my father was adept at holding the *siddur* with one hand, leaving the pinkie from the other free to pop into any crying baby's mouth, as sort of a rabbinic pacifier.

The Ark in the new temple building in Peoria, Illinois had a beautiful curtain that parted in the center, operated by a motor. Inside, the congregation's three *Torah* scrolls rested against a background of black glass, lit only from above with a spotlight pointing down over each scroll. Those lights faded up slowly as the curtain opened. When the Ark curtain began to close, the lights faded out. Very impressive. The lectern was several steps away from the Ark and had a button to activate the Ark's electronics. A second button was inside the Ark to perform the same function when it was time to close it.

As with any new building, there were things that needed additional work, the Ark being one of them. During services, my father would instruct the congregation to rise as the Ark opened. He would press the button on the lectern, then turn to walk to the Ark. Due to extra slack in the curtain's cord that ran through the motor, there was a delay in the opening of the curtain. He would be halfway to the Ark before movement began. For the first several weeks, the whispering was *intense*, "Did you see that? Did you *see that?* The Rabbi merely *looks* at the Ark and it opens!" And, conversely, "The Rabbi just *walks away* from the Ark, and it closes! Have you ever seen *anything* like it?"

You have my permission to "borrow" my father again. I truly hope that you enjoy reading these pages as much as he enjoyed writing them.
And please, don't call him "Sir."

Scott Mahrer, Egg Harbor Township, New Jersey

Foreword

When I think of Rabbi Larry Mahrer, I think of Jewish summer camp, of creative educational programming, of a person dedicated to his family. I can see him on water skis skimming across Lac La Belle or singing, "Dem Bones Gonna Rise Again" in the camp dining room. Jewish educational summer camp and Larry go together like a horse and carriage. When I think of Rabbi Larry Mahrer, I think of high school youth group retreats. When I think of Rabbi Larry, I picture a maverick who questioned authority and liked to think for himself. I think of a rabbi on the pulpit speaking about controversial topics. A rabbi with a gleam in his eye.

I met Rabbi Larry Mahrer the summer of 1964 at Union Institute in Oconomowoc Wisconsin. I was fresh out of high school, learning the ins and outs of camp counseling while Rabbi Mahrer (always Larry) was a member of the camp's faculty. We hit it off from the start. I guess because our relationship centered on camp, I never considered Larry to be my rabbi. He and I were friends. Strange now that I think of it. I was just an eighteen-year-old kid and Larry was a husband, father, and rabbi. But that didn't seem to matter. What did matter was, we were friends. That's a testament to Larry's warmth, humor, and people skills.

Over the years we shared many things. In 1966 I was the camp's sailing instructor. By that time Larry had taught me to water ski, and that summer I taught him and his wife, Jan to sail. Larry continued his love of sailing for many, many years, as did I. I visited the Mahrers in their home in Peoria, Illinois, during my years at the University of Illinois. It was there that Larry introduced me to one of the loves of my life, Ella Fitzgerald and her music. We shared our love of jazz and while doing so always talked into the wee hours.

Back at camp in Wisconsin in 1966, I found myself, now a senior counselor and in charge of the camp's *refet* (barn), along with the sailing program. On one particular day, I had been asked to bring the camp's goat to some unit's program for whatever reason. I took the goat out and tied him to a fence and went back to close the barn. I didn't know that a camp staff member's St Bernard had gotten loose and had run away. When I came out of the barn, I saw the dog attacking the goat. I tried to chase him away but couldn't stop it from attacking. Without getting into the gory details, the dog killed the goat and then lumbered off.

I was distraught. The goat was dead, and I had no idea what to do. I went right to Larry and told him the story. He comforted me, put his arm around me, and led me back to the barn. At the barn he just said, "Let's get a couple of shovels." Together we buried the animal. Having Larry to go to softened the trauma of the moment. We took care of business and life went on.

In 1968 I was the camp's Waterfront Director. As such I arrived at camp very early that summer to set up the waterfront. This was an enormous task, as all the equipment and boats were stored in the camp's warehouse. I never considered that even the piers and platforms were stored. I arrived at camp and the waterfront was bare. I went up to the warehouse and everything had just been piled in a heap. I was overwhelmed. For some reason Larry was already at camp, so of course, I went to Larry. I told him I didn't know where to start. He said, "Find the truck and flatbed. I'll meet you at the warehouse." I just needed a push in the right direction. Larry helped me locate the pier foundations, put them in order by size, and load them on the flatbed along with the pier planks. That was all I needed. I drove them down to the lake and started building the pier one piece at a time. Larry always pointed me in the right direction.

These are just examples of how Larry helped others. They are not about Judaism, but they are about being a rabbi. Larry is the kind of rabbi who rolls up his sleeves and goes to work, solves problems, and helps others. He isn't a, "You should do this" kind of rabbi. Rather he is a, "Let's do this" rabbi. Larry always was and still is a people helper. He has had a most positive impact on many who would go on to become rabbis, myself included. I also went on to become a Camp Director at one of our Union for Reform Judaism camps for thirty-seven years. Larry taught me what I needed to learn at a particularly important time in my life.

He taught me to take the first step. He taught me to respond to the moment and come up with a plan. He taught me to act and to help. I never forgot those lessons.

Larry and I would meet up at every URJ biennial until he retired and then I retired. We don't see much of each other these days. Nevertheless, Larry was a great help to me in those younger days, and we've remained friends all these years. Along with all those life lessons, we skied, and sailed, and we laughed a whole lot.

Rabbi Ron Klotz, Bloomington, Indiana

"I Always Knew You Weren't Really God"

and Other Tales of an Ordinary Rabbinate

Preface

I am certain that I am not much different from most other rabbis in that the events described in this book could have happened during the careers of colleagues. However, because they happened to me, they are important to me and lead me to want to share them with a wider audience.

I grew up in Cleveland, Ohio, in a very active Jewish family, but not a particularly observant one. The earliest job that I can remember my mother holding was as the Executive Director of the Cleveland Chapter of Hadassah. Dad had been involved with the overnight camping program of the Jewish community since the middle 1920s. As I was growing up, he served as the chairperson of the Camp Committee of the Council Educational Alliance, which ran Camp Wise and Camp Henry Baker. Eventually all of this merged into the JCC, and Dad continued to serve as chairman of the Camp Committee and Vice President of the JCC well into his middle sixties. My father was known as "Uncle Hugo" to at least three generations of Clevelanders who at one time or another had either been campers or staff members at Camp Wise in Painesville, Ohio. The camp eventually moved and is now known as Camp Wise at Halle Park near Burton, Ohio. I had the sad pleasure of dedicating the Camp Chapel in memory of my father on August 1, 1975. The outdoor facility is called the "Hugo Mahrer Chapel." Additionally, the very next year, the "Rose and Hugo Mahrer Leadership Development Institute" was created in my parents' names. The Institute is designed to enrich leadership training programs by conducting an orientation weekend for younger staff members before camp opens every June.

In addition, my folks were active with Jewish Vocational service, Jewish Big Brothers, Bellefaire, and other Jewish organizations in the community. It seems as if every night after they came home from work and we had dinner, one or both would run out to go somewhere, to some kind of Jewish meeting. My children would say that my life, as they were growing up, was exactly the same. They were cheated, and now I know it. They felt it as kids, I didn't.

My parents never had a *mezuzah* on their door until I bought them one when they were in their sixties. I cannot remember the observance of any holiday in our home, though we did spend most holidays with my maternal grandparents. We observed the holidays, semi-orthodox style, with the extended family. Mom and Dad did attend services on *Erev Shabbat* in the congregation that used to be called Euclid Avenue Temple, or "Brickner's," to differentiate it from "Silver's" which was only about 25 blocks up Euclid Avenue and a slight turn to the left. My childhood and teen years were spent in a rather peculiar environment that had an intense identification with secular Jewish life, a very strong identification with our Reform congregation, and virtually no religious Jewishness within our home. Maybe my choice of a career in the rabbinate was an unconscious desire to fill in that void.

The tales that I will tell are true, however at times the names have been changed to protect the innocent. Sometimes the names have been changed to protect the not-so-innocent. Wherever it seems proper, the names of actual colleagues and congregants will be used.

Strange things, funny things, sad things, poignant things, and even regular things happen to all people. Possibly because our lives as pulpit clergy put us into such intense contact with people, some of the stories begin to take on a life of their own. I have two motivations for writing this book. Firstly, I have really enjoyed my professional life. I have derived a great deal of pleasure from it and hope that I have made some sort of meaningful contribution to the individuals and the congregations whom I have served. By writing the book, I thought I might be able to share that joy with others. Secondly, some of the things that happened to me might be unique or, at least, instructive. If it hadn't been for Sylvan Schwartzman, all my classmates and I would have left Hebrew Union College-Jewish Institute of Religion (HUC–JIR) in June 1959 without even one iota of an idea about functioning as rabbis. We might have known how to conjugate a verb in the *Pi'el*, but nobody other than Schwartzman ever attempted to help us understand what a rabbi really does. Therefore, some of these tales might be instructive to a younger generation of colleagues. Maybe a mistake that I made in Battle Creek, Michigan, Kenosha, Wisconsin, Peoria, Illinois, St. Louis, Missouri, Wausau, Wisconsin, Topeka, Kansas, Florence, South Carolina or in Dothan, Alabama, will save another young rabbi from a similar misstep.

My thanks to Ann Kuykendall, devoted secretary of Temple Emanu-El, Dothan, Alabama, for all her assistance and particularly for her expertise on the computer. When I was a kid growing up and when dad and I had discussions about things, I frequently would say to him, "What could you possibly know? You were born in the last century!" I was only partially kidding. When I would walk into Ann's office, I would sometimes feel as if I fit the description I gave to my Dad. I'm not even sure that I knew how to turn her computer on. My thanks are also extended to two friends, Mary Goree and Kathleen Nemish. Both have been very helpful by reading the manuscript, talking to me about the concepts I was attempting to describe, and making many valuable and helpful suggestions. All three of these women have my gratitude. Finally, thank you to my son Scott, who digitized and edited the typewritten manuscript for this book twelve years after it was written. What you read today is the final product.

Shabbat On Thursday? and Other Pre-Rabbinic Stories

In the fall of 1955, somebody in the inner workings of the Cincinnati campus of HUC-JIR had the grace to assign me to Rabbi Jerome Folkman of Temple Israel in Columbus, Ohio, as his High Holiday assistant. I took the train to Columbus and Rabbi Folkman met me at the station. Even though I was born and raised in Ohio and had attended undergraduate school at Ohio University, I had never really seen Columbus. Therefore, Rabbi Folkman took me on a brief walking tour of downtown. As we were moving along High Street, he suddenly pointed out a young woman and a child coming toward us. He told me that they were members of the congregation and we would stop and talk for a moment. Jerry greeted the mother and talked to the little boy who appeared to be about three years old. He introduced me to both and told the little boy that when he came to services the following morning for *Rosh HaShanah*, I would be the "rabbi" who would be conducting that service. As the conversation continued between the three of us, the little boy reached up and tugged on Jerry's jacket. Four or five times the little boy interrupted us, and each time Jerry would turn to the boy and very politely ask him what he wanted. Each time the boy would say, "Rabbi why are you here?" and each time Jerry would explain that he had picked me up at the railroad station. The boy continued to yank on Jerry's jacket or pants or fingers and it became very obvious that the railroad station wasn't the answer to the question that the little boy seemed to be asking. Finally, Jerry bent his knees, squatted down to the little boy's eye level and asked him, "What do you really want to know? I have already told you why I am here on the street with Rabbi Mahrer and with your mother and with you. What do you really want to know?" The little boy looked him right in the eye and said, "Why aren't you at the Temple where God is?" I have thought about that little boy many, many times in the intervening forty plus years. I frequently wonder why many congregants are surprised to see rabbis in everyday situations and circumstances. I know that people are surprised to see me walking through the mall and even more so pushing a cart through the grocery store (I was almost tempted to say "buggy" as they do here in Dixie). Why is it so difficult for our congregants to understand that rabbis are humans who have chosen a specific profession and while our humanness may be a little different from theirs, we are also just like them?

After we left the little boy and his mother, Rabbi Folkman and I went directly to the Temple. Following a very brief tour, he took me into the Sanctuary, up on the *bimah* and asked me to open the Union Prayer Book to any page that I desired and to read something to him in both Hebrew and English. As I prepared for my audition, he quickly moved to the rear of the Sanctuary. After I had read two sentences of English, he stopped me and told me to find something to read in Hebrew. Again, a line or two was enough. As he came back to the *bimah* he told me that the student who had been with him the previous year had walked onto the *bimah* on *Erev Rosh HaShanah*, stepped forward to the lectern and absolutely froze. He was unable to conduct the service and Jerry wanted to be sure that I could at least open my mouth and get the words out.

The following year for the High Holidays, I was assigned to a small congregation in Kentucky. I think it would be best if the town were unnamed. Before going to the community, I received a phone call from someone in the congregation asking me if I could blow *shofar*. When I said yes, he was relieved because the congregant who usually assumed that ritual honor was not well. They were very pleased that I would be able to fill in. However, when I arrived and brought my *shofar* into their Sanctuary, problems immediately arose. I was told that my *shofar* could not be used, that it was not proper and not "real." I must admit that I did not understand any of what was happening, nor could I imagine what was improper or unreal about my *shofar*. They were at a loss in terms of explaining the problem further, but one man agreed to find the synagogue's *shofar* and bring it to me so that I could understand what was wrong with mine. He returned in about 20 minutes. I had used the time productively to arrange the lectern to my satisfaction and check that the *Sefer Torah* was rolled properly for *Rosh HaShanah* morning. The gentleman returned to the sanctuary with a beautiful velvet bag in his hand on which the word *shofar* had been lovingly embroidered in Hebrew letters. It was clearly a homemade bag, but one that been done with artistic taste and significant feeling and commitment. In front of a group that now numbered six or seven, he proudly produced a *shofar* with a silver colored trumpet mouthpiece firmly attached. From their point of view, that was a "real" *shofar* and mine was some sort of obvious fake.

The synagogue was over sixty years old and the congregation had existed for about a decade before it was built. In all that time no one could remember a *shofar* without a mouthpiece. In other words, no resident of that community or member of that congregation had ever seen a real *shofar*. Isn't it amazing how often we assume that what we know about Judaism equates to authenticity? We all have our own *minhagim* (customs) in our congregations, but I hope we understand that they are customs and traditions that are particular to our individual congregations, and not representative of generic Judaism or even necessarily of Reform. The following story is somewhat similar. I don't have the slightest idea as to the source of the story I am about to relate, but it has been part of my repertoire for many, many years.

There was once an American Jew who traveled extensively because of business. It was his practice to arrange his schedule so that he could always visit in a synagogue for services. He was particularly attracted to the synagogues of Eastern Europe and the Balkans. On one trip, he stayed over an extra day so that he could worship with the congregation on *Shabbat* morning. As people were called to the *bimah*, in the center of the synagogue, for *Aliyot*, he noticed that each one bent over as he approached the *bimah*. It looked as if all were bowing. He assumed that since the country in which he was visiting was predominantly Catholic, the Jews had picked up the practice of bowing, much the way Catholics will genuflect as they approach the altar. Following the service, he attempted to discover the reason for this behavior and finally was told that once upon a time, before electricity, a low hanging candle chandelier had occupied that space in the aisle, and it was necessary to duck underneath it. The chandelier was long gone, but the "ducking" behavior remained. I find that this is very typical of the usual conservatism in human behavior, especially religious behavior.

In a similar vein, a congregant emailed the following story to me in June 1998. It is reproduced exactly as I received it.

During a service at an old synagogue in Eastern Europe, when the *Sh'ma* was said, half the congregants stood up and half remained sitting. The half that was seated started yelling at those standing to sit down, and the ones standing yelled at the ones sitting to stand up. The rabbi, learned as he was in the Law and commentaries, didn't know what to do. The old Cantor suggested the Rabbi

consult a housebound 103-year-old man, who was
one of the original founders of the congregation.
The rabbi hoped the elderly man would be able to
tell him what the actual synagogue tradition was.
So, he went to the nursing home with a
representative of each faction of the congregation.
The one whose followers stood during *Sh'ma* said to
the old man, "is the tradition to stand during the
prayer?" The old man answered, "No, that is not the
tradition." The one whose followers sat asked, "Is
the tradition to sit during the *Sh'ma*?" The old man
replied, "No, that is not the tradition." Then the
rabbi said to the old man, "The congregants fight all
the time yelling at each other about whether they
should sit or stand." The old man interrupted,
exclaiming: "That is the tradition!"

My next High Holiday assignment was with a congregation in
Pennsylvania which shall also remain unnamed. It seems that one
family had always hosted the student rabbi who came to town for
Rosh HaShanah and *Yom Kippur*. Unfortunately, these people were
now quite aged and probably should not have been permitted to
continue with this responsibility. I was taken to their home in the
middle of the afternoon of *Erev Rosh HaShanah*, shown to a
bedroom upstairs, directed to the bathroom, and given my
towels. After I had cleaned up and put my things away, I came
downstairs to find the couple sound asleep in their chairs in the
living room. I walked into the kitchen to discover that nothing
seemed to be in preparation for dinner. To make a long story

short, I ended up conducting services that evening on an empty stomach and quickly planned for someone to pick me up the following morning for breakfast. It obviously made no impression on the congregation. On *Yom Kippur* I again stayed with that couple and again had no dinner prior to my fast.

My next and final student pulpit was B'nai Abraham in Portsmouth, Ohio. I served that congregation for two and a half years. The first year and a half I was the Educational Director while Jack Spiro served as rabbi. Then, after Jack was ordained, I became the rabbi and Danny Fogel became the Educational Director. I am not certain how long the dual student rabbi system continued in that congregation, but it certainly was a wonderful learning experience for me. When I originally met Jack and Marilyn Spiro, it was the first time that I had ever met people who were born and raised in the south. I never realized how parochial my upbringing had been. On one occasion, when we were playing Scrabble together, Jack built on letters already on the board and ended up with a word spelled T-U-M-A. Obviously, that didn't spell any word with which I was familiar and so I called him on it. With a voice tinged with disbelief he said something like, "You know, Tuma, Tuma, like when you have canca." Obviously, he meant tumor. I don't know whether he was teasing this Yankee or not. I don't know whether he really thought the word was spelled the way he pronounced it. He certainly convinced me that night, however.

On Sundays I would drive to Portsmouth early in the morning, picking up two students on my way in a little town along the Ohio River. I ran the Religious School, which at that time had approximately 30 students in it. I occasionally did some work with the Youth Group early in the afternoon and then returned to Cincinnati. I did that every week that Religious School was in session. The senior Student Rabbi came to Portsmouth on alternate Friday afternoons and conducted services Friday night, made hospital and home visits on Saturday, and occasionally conducted some adult education activities on Saturday. Then he would return to Cincinnati. The senior Student Rabbi was always in the fifth year at HUC, and the Educational Director was a fourth-year student.

The family whose children I would drive were typical for the 1950s. I visited them for breakfast every Sunday morning and occasionally for lunch on Sunday afternoons. The wife didn't work, and the husband owned a retail store. As I remember, he sold basically soft goods, clothing, linens, etc. Because the community was so small, and because it was the first town of any size west of Portsmouth, his store was the only one of its kind. His busiest times were Friday night and Saturday as people came in from surrounding communities and farms to do their weekly shopping. I knew all of this, and likewise knew the family never attended services at the synagogue in Portsmouth on Friday night. Therefore, I was very surprised over breakfast one Sunday to hear a conversation about how the family had celebrated *Shabbat* and how the younger child, a son, had finally agreed that he would recite *Kiddush* all alone. The father told me how pleased he was with the knowledge his son had gained in our Religious School. I expressed my thanks and simply let it go. I kept wondering about how the family observed *Shabbat* when everybody was so busy tending to business at the store. The same subject came up on a Sunday morning a couple of weeks later, and it was then that I discovered that the family observed *Shabbat* at the dinner table on Thursday evening. Somehow my good sense prevailed and I didn't say to the family, "You can't do that!"

I must admit that I really thought the family was wrong. I believed that other arrangements could have been made so that *Shabbat* could have been welcomed into the family on Friday night. I believed that individual people and families didn't have the right to make such dramatic changes in Judaism. Now, I am no longer quite so positive. The "*Shabbat*" which those children had might have taught a variety of lessons. Since I never knew the family that well, and since I was never with them on Thursday night, I don't know how it was handled. But, in retrospect, it appears to me that the lesson which the children learned might have been that *Shabbat* is so important that it needs to be a part of the life experience of every Jewish family. Thus, it might be necessary to make some adjustments as to when it is observed, all the while realizing that *Shabbat* really is from sundown Friday to sundown Saturday. That can be construed as a very positive lesson about *Shabbat*. On the other hand, the children may have learned that Judaism is whatever we make it: that we can change, adapt, or adopt it to become anything that is convenient to us and that Judaism makes absolutely no demands on us. You might say, the message of that lesson is that Judaism is whatever you want it to be, which I take to be a very negative and destructive view on Judaism. I only wish that I had thought about these things twenty or more years ago, so that I could have attempted to follow up with those two youngsters to see how they handled *Shabbat* and the rest of Judaism in their adult lives. It would have been interesting to discover whether the lessons taught by "*Shabbat* on Thursday" helped produce a positive and meaningful Judaism in their adult lives or not.

The sanctuary in Portsmouth was built with a balcony across the back and a choir loft above and behind the Ark. Each of those areas had a round stained-glass window which could be opened by swiveling the window on its center post. In the years prior to my serving as a student rabbi, on *Yom Kippur* morning the members of the choir, who were all Christians from the community, would simply get up at the end of the *Torah* service, walk down the back stairs, and leave the building until they were expected to return for the Afternoon service. I asked them if they would please remain seated in the choir loft until services were fully over. I suggested that it just didn't look right for them to walk out while I was delivering my sermon. I told them that it gave the wrong impression and might encourage congregants to walk out as well. The choir members understood, and it presented no problem to them. *Yom Kippur* was a very warm day, and in the building that was not air-conditioned, the windows in the choir loft and in the balcony had been opened. About ten minutes into my sermon, I noticed some strange facial motions from members of the congregation. I then noticed a slight, unexpected, and peculiar odor. Within a few seconds it all became very clear; most of us were smiling and a few were laughing out loud. It seems that the members of the choir, now required to stay in the choir loft for an extra twenty to twenty-five minutes, had very quietly opened their thermos bottles and were enjoying (I hope) my sermon while drinking their coffee. Those of us who were fasting for the holiday found the aroma of coffee to be extraordinarily pleasant and more than tempting.

My daughter, Debi, was born in July 1955. The following spring, when she was about nine months old, we noticed an article in the newspaper to the effect that the Cincinnati Conservatory, which was a magnificent series of greenhouses, was about to open their annual Easter display. Since it was one of our favorite places, and since we did not want to go on a weekend when it would be extra crowded, I decided to take a day off school so my wife and I could take Debi to the Conservatory. I can't even begin to remember what excuse I was going to use the following day when I met with my professors. But I soon discovered that it didn't make any difference. The next morning, on the front page of one of the sections of the newspaper, was a very large picture of the three of us admiring the Easter lilies and the other flowers on the opening day of the exhibit. Obviously, everyone at HUC knew exactly where I had been the day before.

The following story was related by Phil Gershon, who was in his final year of rabbinic school during my first. We lived near each other in the same apartment development. His biweekly congregation was somewhere in eastern Iowa. As was typical, he was invited for *Shabbat* dinner in the home of a congregant prior to services on Friday night. As he sat on the couch in the living room, talking to the husband while the wife made final dinner preparations, he did what many of us do. He put his arm along the top of the back of the couch. Much to his surprise, his fingers touched something rather prickly. When he looked over the edge of the couch, he discovered what he had felt. He saw a fully decorated Christmas tree which had been hidden because the "rabbi" was coming to dinner. He laughed about that experience at least until the time of his ordination the following June, and for all I know, he is still laughing or smiling. Oh well! Another story. Another experience. Another fun time in Judaism.

We Were Teenage Rabbis

My first pulpit was Temple Beth El in Battle Creek, Michigan. I arrived shortly after the first of July, and by mid-August I was on my way to a camp just outside of Detroit to be a member of the faculty for a Michigan State Temple Youth (MSTY) conclave. With all the changes recently made in the North American Federation for Temple Youth (NFTY), I don't know if MSTY even exists any longer as a separate entity.[1] However, in those days it included all the Youth Groups of Reform congregations in

---

[1] In 1994, the North American Federation for Temple Youth (NFTY) was renamed as the Reform Jewish Youth Movement, keeping the NFTY acronym. The Michigan State Temple Youth (MSTY), a region of NFTY, was renamed at that time to NFTY Michigan (NFTY-MI). All of the other regions of NFTY were similarly renamed to create a greater connection to the North American movement. The original names and acronyms have been maintained in this book as they are historically accurate for the period described.

Michigan as well as South Bend, Indiana. But, before we continue with this adventure, it is time for another story.

In October 1957, my second child named Jeff was born. Shortly after his birth, probably around 6:00 a.m., I attempted to visit him and his mother at Jewish Hospital in Cincinnati. I confidently parked my car, opened the front door, walked through the lobby, and began to move into the hospital when a huge black arm came out of the doorway and stopped me in my tracks. The rest of the body soon followed, and I was rather pointedly asked, "Where do you think you're going?" My reply was that I was going to see my wife and my son who had been born within the last hour. I was very politely told that I could not visit anybody in the hospital because I wasn't yet sixteen years old and hospital rules required visitors to be a minimum of sixteen. Intelligence wasn't my strong point that morning and I attempted to explain that I was going to see my wife and my child. I was firmly told that I wasn't going anywhere because I wasn't old enough and, furthermore, who in the hell did I think I was? That remark caught my attention and I found my driver's license and showed it to the security guard and was permitted, finally, to visit Jeff.

The purpose of the story is to give you some idea as to how I looked at age twenty-five and a half, and how I still looked on my way to that camp conclave a little less than two years later. Michigan State Temple Youth had the wonderful advantage of women from the Sisterhood region serving as advisors and helpers. They attended every function, did much of the background work, and many of the jobs that no one else would want to do. Their presence and their level of activity accounted for the success of MSTY, and helped it to become one of the more active and more stable regions of what was then called the National Federation of Temple Youth. A couple of these Sisterhood women have gone on to very prominent roles with Women of Reform Judaism and the Union for Reform Judaism. They have been Board members of both organizations, and possibly even officers. In fact, one of them named Lillian Maltzer was a member of the National Board of the URJ representing the Southeast Council until her recent death (at the time of this writing). She resided in Longboat Key, Florida, and I have had the privilege of spending time with her at many recent national and regional biennials. She is greatly missed.

When I arrived at the camp ahead of the buses bringing the kids, I was met by some of the Sisterhood women and simply identified myself as Larry Mahrer from Battle Creek. I then began to wander around, looking over the facilities of the camp and attempting to see how the camp layout, equipment, and facilities might be usable in our programming. It wasn't too long before I heard the noise of teenagers and I realized that the buses had arrived. I went to join everybody and noticed that the kids were standing in various lines to collect the materials that they would need for the conclave, as well as their specific housing assignments. When the kids had moved off, one of the ladies came and said to me, "I'm sorry, but on our list of campers we only have girls from Battle Creek. Isn't that where you are from?" I replied in the affirmative and suggested that they look on their faculty list for Rabbi Larry Mahrer and I was certain that they would find my name there. Clearly, they were highly embarrassed. Since I have already told you that I looked very young, I will now add that I was 5'-8" tall, weighed approximately 120 pounds, and had what I called a butch haircut, which meant that it was only about a quarter of an inch long at the longest. I again had been mistaken for a kid.

But I must have functioned adequately as a rabbi, because part way through the conclave I was asked if I would be willing to assume the responsibility of becoming the Rabbinic Advisor to MSTY. I immediately accepted. To some extent at least, being young and looking like a teenager worked to my advantage. On many occasions I really got to know the kids before they knew that I was a rabbi. In fact, many of the teenagers who had previously attended functions with me stood on the sidelines to watch and see how first-timers would react to me. It was always the same. The teenagers who didn't know me assumed that I was one of them.

Many, many, many years later while Rabbi Danny Syme was one of the vice presidents of the URJ, he visited my congregation to be the speaker at an important congregational dinner. He began by informing my congregants that he had always remembered me as the "sports car rabbi," though this was the first time he had ever used the words in my presence. It stems from the fact that when I was at the camp with the kids from MSTY, in 1959 and subsequent years, I drove a Peugeot 403. Danny, growing up in Detroit and long before car ownership, must have felt that it was peculiar for a rabbi to be driving a car from France.

I am rather certain that his father, a prominent Detroit rabbi, drove a car created by the Big Three. Danny was, of course, a MSTY-ite during those years.

The downside of looking that way was that many of the adults with whom I came in contact, my own congregants as well as members of the congregations who hosted various MSTY events, likewise reacted to me as a teenager and then were apologetic to discover that I was a rabbi. My very first experience like that was within the first two or three weeks after my arrival in Battle Creek. A member of the congregation whom I had not met walked into the building and came to my office. My door was open, but he rapped on it nonetheless. When I looked up and said hello, his opening words were, "Hi. Is your dad around? I am looking for the Rabbi." Clearly, in that instance I was my own dad and the rabbi. Of course, he was embarrassed even after I attempted to point out to him that many people assumed that I was a teenager rather than twenty-seven years old and the father of two children.

David Baylinson always told me that he had many such experiences during the early days of his rabbinic career. We were friends at HUC in Cincinnati even though David was a year ahead of me. When I arrived in Battle Creek, he had already served one year as the assistant rabbi of Temple Beth El in Detroit and was highly active with his congregation's Youth Group and MSTY. In fact, the title of this chapter was supposed to have been the title of the book that David and I were planning to write in the early 1960s. Like many such brilliant ideas, it never got off the ground, but I use it here with fond memories and in tribute to David. David presently is Rabbi Emeritus of Temple Beth Or of Montgomery, Alabama, and we are both very pleased that we have rekindled our friendship. We attempt to have lunch together once a month. What follows are a series of stories which David relates from the early part of his career when he might have looked more like a teenager than I did. These were to have been in the book we planned to write over 50 years ago:

> With my last name beginning with "B," I was the first member of the Freshman Class to be assigned a Sabbath service at the nearby Home for the Aged. With prayer book in hand and *Torah* portion well-rehearsed, I entered the Chapel, stood at the pulpit, and before I uttered one Hebrew word someone in the back cried out: "Who's the boy up there? We're supposed to have a Rabbi!" It took me a moment to recover after the Director said: "But he is the Rabbi."

> My first Student Congregation was in New Bern, North Carolina. I was in my second year at Hebrew Union College. I was twenty-four years old, married, and was too often taken as a seventeen-year-old. To give you an idea, my wife and I were refused a drink on our honeymoon in New York where the legal drinking age was nineteen. When I arrive in New Bern, I began the obligatory walk down the main street to visit the merchants and

introduce myself. I walked into one store and introduced myself to the owner, who called upstairs to his wife to come and meet the Rabbi. She was halfway down the stairs when she stopped dead and said: "THAT'S the Rabbi?" As much as I tried to smile, it was difficult. After that, as soon as I walked into a store or home, I immediately announced who I was.

Sometimes it wasn't looking young but being young and inexperienced that led to humbling events. My biweekly congregation was in Anniston, Alabama. Never in my wildest dreams did I believe that I would spend over 35 years in Montgomery, Alabama, just 90 miles south of Anniston. Part of the weekend was spent visiting the sick at home and in the hospital. I spent some time visiting a woman named Daisy who was totally non-communicative because of her illness. I went back the following day and the nurses were all smiles because Daisy was responding to the medicine and so much better. I went into the room and we had a lovely chat. Then Daisy asked me to say the 23rd Psalm for her. I began, Daisy took my hand, and having never been to a funeral nor in the presence of death, Daisy died holding my hand. I had to plan for the funeral, conduct the funeral even though I had never attended one, and console members of the congregation. I may not have looked any older, but believe me, I was older and more experienced very quickly.

My very first congregation was Temple Beth El in Detroit, Michigan. I had been at Beth El for only a few weeks when I performed my first wedding. It took place in a hotel and I was asked to dress in a tuxedo. I am a stickler for promptness and when the wedding director didn't start on time, I went up to him and said I wanted the wedding to begin in two minutes. He took one look at me and said, "Don't get smart, sonny, we don't start until the Rabbi comes."

He stuttered and stammered an apology, and after that we became good friends. I was very happy when Beth El Rabbis began to wear robes so I could be identified.

I have very fond memories of Detroit and MSTY. One year at camp I was the Advisor and it was my duty, along with the Sisterhood Advisor, to check the cabins and make sure everyone was in bed at the end of the day. Ruth checked the girls' side, I the boys'. When we met, Ruth said one girl was missing. I said one boy was missing and we both realized that they were "going together." We scoured the camp but found no one. Our irritation changed to fear. Finally, we went over to the younger children's camp, which was off limits. We saw the two innocently swinging on the swings, oblivious to everything. They will never forget my outburst, "Now that you've found it's so much fun swinging together, why don't you try going to bed." It came to haunt me for many years.

I remember a *Shabbat* evening service in Grand Rapids, Michigan, at the beginning of a MSTY Conclave. Following the service, along with everyone else, I moved from the sanctuary into the Social Hall for the *Oneg Shabbat*. As I approached the table, I asked the hostess for a cup of coffee and she indicated that there was milk at the other end of the table. I responded, "No, I really would like a cup of coffee." She pointed through a doorway and said that the coke machine was down the hall. When I asked her why on two occasions she had denied my request for coffee, she told me that it was the policy of their congregation not to provide coffee to teens. I then asked, "Even if the teenager is really a rabbi?" Unfortunately, she never understood the implication of that question and I simply had to tell her that I was the rabbi from Battle Creek, the Regional Youth Advisor, not a teenager, and was therefore entitled to a cup of coffee. The following morning, services were held just for the MSTYites who were attending the Conclave. At the end of the service, I announced that discussion groups would follow immediately and told the kids which room would house which group. That meant that I was one of the last to leave the sanctuary and walk into the Social Hall. I was speaking with the host rabbi when, once again, I was confronted by a motherly type from the synagogue membership. She very promptly and politely patted me on my fanny and told me to move along because it was time for me to be in class. The host rabbi asked her whether it was her practice to lovingly pat rabbis on the fanny, and if it was, how come she had never done it to him?

I continued to be the Rabbinic Advisor to MSTY until I left Battle Creek at the end of March 1962. I went to Beth Hillel Temple in Kenosha, Wisconsin, a little earlier than usual because they had no rabbi but did have a Confirmation Class, whereas the congregation in Battle Creek had a rabbi but no Confirmands. I continued my involvement with Youth Group and very soon was asked to be the Regional Advisor to the Northern Federation of Temple Youth (NoFTY)[2]. NoFTY covered northern Illinois except for Chicago, all of Wisconsin, Minnesota, the Dakotas, and a very narrow eastern strip of Iowa. The then URJ camp in Oconomowoc, Wisconsin, was our headquarters. The Region met at the camp in early June and then again during the midwinter break from school in December. There weren't too many similar experiences with NoFTY, partly because we were almost always at camp and partly because I now had a third child, had passed my 30th birthday, and my family came to camp with me. I assume that all those things contributed to a somewhat more mature look, if not behavior.

---

[2] In 1994, NoFTY was renamed to NFTY Northern (NFTY-NO).

We Were Rabbis For Teenagers

When people ask me why I became a rabbi, or how I decided that the rabbinate would be my career choice, I frequently answer that when I was early in my teen years, I met rabbis who had a very profound influence on me. I think that what I really meant was that I met rabbis who accepted me as a real person. Even though I was a teenager, they treated me with the same respect and dignity that they would show to an adult. They convinced me by their behavior that they truly had my interests at heart. Lastly, they demonstrated in innumerable ways that Judaism mattered to them. In 1947, a rabbi on staff at my family's congregation in Cleveland named Sam Silver took me with him to Camp Lake of the Woods, in Decatur, Michigan. This was either the first or second of NFTY's National Leadership Institutes. There, I met people like Ellie Schwartz and Gene Borowitz who ran the program. Both went on to impressive careers in the service of Reform Judaism: Ellie, as the Executive Director of NFTS, and

Gene as a prominent rabbi, author, thinker, and longtime member of the faculty of Hebrew Union College-Jewish Institute of Religion in New York.

While I had been a camper every summer from age seven on and a member of camp staff or administration from age fourteen on, I had never been part of a program that focused exclusively on teenagers and on Judaism. I was mightily impressed and totally committed. Most important, I met adults who truly cared about kids. I cannot overemphasize how important that was in my maturation and in my eventual career choice.

At that Institute I met a teenager from Erie, Pennsylvania, and another from Buffalo, New York. While I cannot remember all the details of who did what or how, I do know that the three of us were instrumental in creating a region of NFTY then known as the Lake Erie Federation of Temple Youth (LEFTY). The girl from Buffalo became its first president and I was its first vice president. As I remember it, we did very well for a newborn region, with three or four very successful regional activities within the first couple of years. That region later became known as the Northeastern Lakes Federation of Temple Youth (NELFTY). The story that made the rounds in Cleveland at the time of the name change was that the bus carrying kids was detained on its way back from a LEFTY conclave in Toronto as it returned through customs at the US. border. It seems that the word "LEFTY" triggered some intense reactions in officials during the days of McCarthyism. The story may not be absolutely accurate, but it certainly sounds plausible given the attitude of such a large segment of our population at that time in our nation's history. At that time, the name was changed.

Maurice Davis was a member of the rabbinic staff of Euclid Avenue Temple in Cleveland who made a profound impact on me. In my formative years, Morrie was by far the most prominent example of a rabbi who cared about kids. In every way, he indicated to us that we were important to him as individuals. He believed that our ideas were worth considering and discussing, even if in the long run they turned out to have little merit or were based on a faulty premise.

One of the other lessons that I learned from Morrie Davis was to accept kids as they were with all their emotions, frequent self-depreciation, open enthusiasm, or their quiet disdain. Morrie taught me that we can't change those aspects of a teenager's life. This was clearly demonstrated one year on the last night of camp. We had gone to the camp chapel up a hill and into the woods for *Havdalah* and for a final "goodbye" service. It had been entirely planned by the kids and was very effective in creating an emotional atmosphere. Morrie and I were among the first to leave the chapel. We were walking very slowly down the hill when one of the girls came up between us crying openly and loudly. With her left hand she held Morrie's hand, with her right hand she held mine, and after walking a little bit with the only sound being her sobs she said, "It's going to be so difficult not to see my friends tomorrow night. It's going to be so difficult to leave camp and to end this wonderful time. I don't think I will ever again be as excited as I have been this week. I am going to miss everyone so much." We kept on walking and she kept on sobbing. Then suddenly she dropped both of our hands and said in a very loud, cheerful voice, "I wonder what we're having for snack?" She ran off down the hill and disappeared into the darkness. As Morrie said, we must accept kids with all their inconsistencies!

By the time I was the student rabbi of the congregation in Portsmouth, Ohio, Morrie was already known nationally as "Moe Dean." This reflected the number of youth group camps and conclaves which he had served as dean. During my years in Cincinnati, he was the rabbi of Temple Adath Israel in Lexington, Kentucky. Our youth groups were both members of the same NFTY region: the Ohio Valley Federation of Temple Youth (OVFTY). On one occasion, at an OVFTY Camp Conclave, we found ourselves standing on opposite sides of a circle of teenagers seated around a campfire. In the glow of those flames, our eyes met and we spontaneously started to move toward each other around that circle behind the kids. We met and without a word we embraced. Without a word we discovered that we both had tears in our eyes. Without a word we separated slightly, looked at each other intently for a while, and then returned to our original places outside the circle behind the kids. I know what I was feeling. It was a deep sense of pleasure, and some pride, that I found myself following in the footsteps of a rabbi for whom I had a great deal of respect and affection. Additionally, there was some measure of surprise that life had brought us back together again, particularly in a setting that was so important to both of us. Lastly, seeing him there sort of validated my own involvement with the teenagers of the student congregation I was serving and the region of which they were a part.

I had no idea exactly how Moe Dean felt that night, and I doubt that I gave it much thought in 1958.Now, I know. As the "older rabbi," I have had similar experiences with colleagues who I once knew as teenagers. Some of them I met through my continuing involvement with both regional and national youth activities, but most of them have come from the URJ camp in Oconomowoc, Wisconsin. The Olin-Sang-Ruby Union Institute is more than just the granddaddy of all URJ camps. It is a breeding ground for Reform Jewish professionals, having been involved in the creation of many rabbis, cantors, educators, and social workers. I served on the rabbinic faculty of that camp consecutively from 1963 through 1973, and again from 1977 through 1981. I have returned on three other occasions. During many of those years in the sixties, I spent the entire summer at camp. At other times, I served on the faculty of URJ camps in Zionsville, Indiana, and Cleveland, Georgia. During the summer of 2005, I served on the faculty of Henry Jacobs Camp in Utica, Mississippi. Another faculty member was Rabbi Gene Levy of Little Rock, Arkansas, who is also an OSRUI alum.

As I look at old photos and movies, and as I think of the young men and women who served on that camp staff and the kids who were our campers, I come across many faces of people who are now my professional colleagues. I am not certain that I had any specific influence on many of them, though I am convinced that the very positive and happy Jewish experiences which we were able to provide in the camp setting had something to do with their choices. However, there are several folks who came from that camp and who do credit me, at least in some measure, with their choice to select a career in Reform Judaism. Rabbi Gary Zola, now the Executive Director of The Jacob Rader Marcus Center of the American Jewish Archives and The Edward M. Ackerman Family Distinguished Professor of the American Jewish Experience & Reform Jewish History at HUC-JIR in Cincinnati, first met me when he was twelve years old. It was amazing how someone who turned out so well could have been so troublesome in his early teen years. Without going into all the details, let's just say that other campers were known to have been better behaved. Nonetheless, when Gary was ordained in Cincinnati in 1982, he asked me to be part of his family for the Ordination service. I was honored to be able to do it and I fully enjoyed all the attendant festivities with the "Cincinnati Red." Gary was our camper, a member of our staff, eventually a member of our faculty, and now a treasured colleague and friend. When you see him next, ask him why he brought a can of Lysol when he stayed in our home on a visit to the congregation in Florence, South Carolina.

Another who followed a similar pattern is Ron Klotz, now retired after 37 years of being the Director of the Goldman Union Camp Institute which is the URJ camp in Zionsville, Indiana. I met Ron when he was part of the Counselor In Training program at OSRUI and worked with him extensively as he became the unit head of the camp program for which I was the rabbinic faculty. Ron taught me to sail on Lac La Belle, introducing me to what has become my lifelong love. It was in Oconomowoc that I purchased the first of the four sailboats that I have owned. Ron was a frequent guest at my house in Kenosha, Wisconsin, sometimes driving up from Champaign, Illinois for a good roast beef meal in the middle of a difficult college semester. At one time or another, all three of my children were part of Ron's camp staff in Indiana. He also officiated the wedding of my youngest son Scott to his wife Nilda in Atlantic City, New Jersey. That was one of the most interesting weddings I have ever attended in that the *Shevah B'rachot* were recited in Hebrew, English, and Spanish in order to accommodate the Spanish speaking portion of Nilda's family. If you can't be creative, you can't cut it in camping! After all these years, Ron and I still treat each other to a beer at URJ Biennials. He owes me one!

Rabbi Robert Ourach, originally of Michigan City, Indiana, is another colleague who was at Oconomowoc. In his young teens he managed to get his hands on one of two walkie talkies that had been brought to camp by the kids. As I was walking around the grounds late one evening, long after lights out, I heard someone in one of the cabins talking. I went in and discovered somebody using the other walkie talkie. I reached out my hand and he gave it to me and almost immediately I heard Bob Ourach's voice talking about one of the girl campers. When he was finished, I pushed the appropriate button and said, "Ourach, this is Rabbi Larry! Get the hell off the radio. Go to sleep. Bring me the radio in the morning." We subsequently became good friends. I taught him to water ski and sail at Oconomowoc and on more than one occasion helped him to recover from excessive exposure to the sun. Some people never learn. Later, after Bob became my colleague, we shared a room at many Central Conference of American Rabbis (CCAR) conventions. He never got over the fact that I would bring my own feather pillow. I guess from his point of view that was an excess.

I don't know how often a brother and a sister both become rabbis, but it happened with Mike Weinberg and Ellen Weinberg Dreyfuss. They were both part of the OSRUI camp family in their teen and young adult years and have both indicated to me in some measure that I influenced their career choice. Both honored me with those comments. I know that when I attend regional or national activities of the URJ or the CCAR, I look forward to once again having the opportunity to spend some time with these colleagues who once were teenagers or staff members at one of the camps where I was a faculty member. Seeing them helps me to understand that my career choice, designed to have an impact on Jews and Judaism, was not only proper but also bore fruit. I love them all. I respect them all. I admire what they do, and I wish them all the very best. They have honored me in so many ways.

As a member of the rabbinic faculty of OSRUI, I always involved myself with other faculty members and with camp staff in a variety of *Kuntzim*, practical jokes. In fact, at one point someone dubbed me *Rosh Vaad Hakuntz* (Head of the Kuntz Committee). One night, someone thought to turn the tables on me. Somewhere around 1:00 a.m., the door to our room opened and something plopped loudly on the floor. When I finally got the light on, I discovered that it was a burlap bag out of which walked a chicken. I must admit that my first thought had to do with the dog who was sleeping at the foot of the bed. I had visions of feathers floating all over the room. As quickly as possible, I picked up the chicken and the burlap bag and threw them both into the hall.

I was later told by two colleagues, who were also members of the faculty, that they had seen the chicken in the hall when they left in the morning to assume their responsibilities. Our resident philosopher named Hillel Gamoran, commented, "There is a chicken in the hallway. There must be a reason for that." The other named Don Splansky obviously knew me fairly well and thought, "There is a chicken in the hall. Larry must be involved in that somehow."

There is another interesting story to tell about Don. He was a member of our staff and faculty all through rabbinic school and was married to Greta Lee, the daughter of our Chicago colleague, Ernst Lorge. This entitled them to live in the Lodge with the rest of the rabbinic faculty. For all those years, when we spent summers together while he was a rabbinic student, he called me Rabbi Mahrer. He arrived at camp for the summer of 1968 immediately after his Ordination. He said hello to me and for the first time called me Larry. I hugged him and thanked him and welcomed him as a new colleague.

In 1960 I was a member of the faculty of a NFTY National Institute at the URJ Camp in Pennsylvania. Subsequently, that camp became known as the Harlam Camp. While I don't remember the specific subject matter of our study theme in 1960, I know that it had something to do with social action. For one evening program, we rearranged the dining hall so that it looked like a lunch counter. Most of the teenage campers were in the audience and as the psychodrama began they were instructed to remain absolutely quiet. One teen was dressed as a waiter and stood behind our make-believe counter. Another teen sat at the counter. We then asked four or five other teens to walk into the restaurant one at a time, sit at the counter, and do whatever seemed appropriate under the circumstances. As each one would sit down, the waiter would approach and say, "What would you like to order for lunch?" Once that line was delivered, the teenager already sitting at the counter said, "Please don't order. He won't serve me because I am a Negro." Obviously, what we were interested in was the reaction of the camper who had just walked into the "restaurant." Somehow, without thinking clearly, we selected a girl from a very small town in Mississippi to be the second subject of this psychodrama. When she was asked not to order by the supposed Negro, she broke into tears. Inadvertently, we had placed her in a very stressful situation, even though she knew that it was make-believe. Clearly the sit-ins and the freedom rides and the bus boycotts had an impact on her life. We stopped the program at that time and talked about her reaction after she gave us permission. It provided a wonderful opportunity for us to help teenagers from all over the country understand how deeply held the feelings were of people who lived in the south. I think it helped some of those teenagers understand the difference between that which is considered to be correct from a moral or intellectual point of view, but contrary to the local culture in terms of emotional content.

At that same Institute I created a sociodrama which had repercussions many years later. The faculty felt that the kids just weren't tuned in and were not really participating at any kind of gut level. So, I turned to outside help.

I drove to town and with the help of the Western Union office, I prepared a fake cablegram addressed to us at camp. I then drove to the Sheriff's department and arranged to have it delivered with lights flashing and sirens blaring sometime between 2:00 and 3:00 in the morning, whenever it was convenient for the deputy who was on duty. The cablegram supposedly was from Rabbi Sam "Cookie" Cook, Director of NFTY, who at the time was in Israel with some of our American kids. The cablegram asked us to discuss a particular issue and to immediately cable our response back because the Israeli teenagers desperately wanted to know what we thought.

Somewhere around 2:30 the next morning, the Sheriff's Deputy came into camp with all the lights on top of the car flashing and with his siren going as loudly as possible. Everybody woke up and came out to see what the problem was. He asked around for Rabbi Mahrer, and when I finally showed up, he hand delivered the fake cablegram to me. In the light of his headlights, I opened it, read it, and showed it to other members of the faculty who obviously already knew exactly what it said. We went through the motions of deciding to hold the discussion immediately since Cookie wanted an immediate response and we were all up anyway. I thanked the Deputy and as he left, whispered instructions to please stop by sometime during the daylight hours to let him know how well the program went. He thought it was a neat idea and was pleased to have been asked to participate.

While some of the faculty made cocoa and found things to eat, the rest of us ran a full discussion of whatever question it was to which Sam wanted an answer. We then found a portable blackboard, rolled it out, and began to write our cabled response. After about an hour or so we were finished. I copied the wording very carefully from the blackboard and promised the kids that I would take it to town to send as a cable the first thing in the morning when the Western Union office opened. Everybody went to bed, and we let the kids sleep an extra hour or so the following morning. That's the end of the story, or at least I thought that was the case.

Donny Mintz had been one of the campers at the Institute that summer. He eventually became the president of the NFTY and ran unsuccessfully for mayor of New Orleans. He was present during the URJ National Biennial conference where we observed the 50th anniversary of NFTY and a significant anniversary in the life of Sam Cook. All of this took place at a special program in the evening. Donny got up to tell all of those assembled how as a teenager he had participated in this very significant event of replying to a cablegram from Sam in Israel. He explained how important it was to him that Sam Cook cared enough to ask

American teenagers for their opinion. He added how thrilled he had been to participate in the discussion which led to a cable back to Israel expressing the opinion of leadership within local Temple Youth Groups from around the country. He described the program in perfect detail; it had made enough of an impression on him so that he remembered all of it. Unfortunately, he never caught on to the fact that the whole program was phony and that the two cables were fakes.

I was sitting right in front of him as he told this story to those assembled to honor NFTY and Sam. I never had the courage to tell him the truth. I don't know if another member of the faculty from that Institute who attended that night clued him in. In any event, if he didn't know the truth before, maybe someone who reads this book will tell him about it. Another NTFYite who was present at that Institute that summer was Marty Frost, who at the time of this writing was a member of Congress from Texas. We certainly did turn out some mighty good adults. I was fortunate enough to have met Rabbi Abraham "Cronnie" Cronbach during my student days in Cincinnati, even though he was no longer a full-time member of the faculty. I realized later that he had been at the 1947 National Leadership Institute which I attended.

In 1961, along with Rabbi Joe Goldman, I served as Co-Dean of a NFTY National Leadership Institute at the URJ camp in Zionsville, Indiana. At the time, Joe was the Associate Director of NFTY. It was then that I had the opportunity of watching Abraham Cronbach work his "magic" with high school Instituters.

I wrote this portion of the book in Orlando, Florida, late in December 1996. During this time, I was a faculty member of the NFTY-SE Winter Regional Conclave (formerly known as SEFTY). The rabbinic advisor at that time was JayR Davis of Vero Beach, Florida. He is Morrie Davis' son and Abraham Cronbach's grandson. Morrie married Cronnie's daughter, Marian. At services on *Erev Shabbat*, JayR included a very brief story about an old man in a three-piece black suit working with teenagers at a National Institute at the camp in Oconomowoc many, many years ago. When services were over, I went to JayR and told him that I recognized the story about his grandfather and how much I respected and loved him. It was a very special moment for me because it validated my memories. It was important for me because I began to understand that things that happened so long ago in my life are still being shared with our Reform Jewish teenagers.

I had heard stories of Cronnie's "magic" with kids at National Institutes, but it wasn't until the summer of 1961 that I saw it in action. He was truly amazing. He would hold 50 or 60 kids in absolute silence for an hour or more on a beautiful *Shabbat* afternoon while he told them a Bible story that always turned out to agree with his pacifistic ideas and concepts. Haman turned out to be misunderstood and generally a pretty decent guy. That is but one example of the way he told stories to our campers. Many of those stories were finally published in book form: *Stories Made From Bible Stories*. For all I know, I have the last copy around. If you happen to come across one somewhere, maybe buried in a synagogue library, take it home and read it. It will give you a wonderful introduction to an absolutely marvelous man.

I had not been a faculty member of a Regional Conclave for over a decade before being asked to serve in 1996. I spent four days with 264 teenagers and a staff of about 45 at a hotel in Orlando, Florida. It was wonderful!

I remember some of my early summers as a faculty member at OSRUI in Oconomowoc when I watched some of my senior colleagues who seemed to have lost touch with the kids. From my perspective, they just did not appear to relate very well to them. I wondered whether I would know if and when I reached that stage. As I drove to Orlando, I began to think about my age and the number of years that I had not been part of programs of this sort. I wasn't sure how well I would do. I must admit that it took several hours before I could really loosen up and get back in the groove of dealing with teenagers in a way that made us all comfortable. Much to my pleasure, I was successful and a great deal of the feedback I received from other staff members and the kids themselves was very positive. I felt comfortable with the contributions that I made to the success of an excellent program and I hoped that I would be given the opportunity to continue that aspect of my professional life. I also hoped that I would know when it was time to quit.

The person primarily responsible for the entire Winter Regional was Jo Ellen Unger, who served as the Regional Director of Junior and Senior High Youth Programming. Though I had served in similar capacities as a volunteer many years previously, I learned a whole new style from Jo Ellen. In addition to being wonderfully organized and charismatic and having a remarkable ability to relate to teenagers, she also functioned in a way that permitted the kids to run much of the activities themselves and make significant program decisions by themselves. As I watched her operate, I became aware of her remarkable ability to empower those teenagers. It was a method of working with youth groups that I had not experienced in any significant way previously. Most of the youth who were in leadership roles took their positions quite seriously and approached their responsibilities with a level of commitment and intelligence that I found to be surprising. Additionally, it was very obvious that the majority of kids in attendance had a great deal of respect for their peer leaders and were able to follow their leadership without some of the boisterousness and general complaining which I had come to expect. They seemed to understand that their leaders were empowered and that the decisions had been made by the kids themselves, not handed down as edicts by adults. That certainly made for a much happier experience with considerably less confusion and much more smoothness, happiness, and pleasure. Thanks, Jo Ellen. You taught me a great deal.

I Also Know I Am Not Isaac Mayer Wise

In the late 1950s when I was a student at the College-Institute in Cincinnati, Jacob Rader Marcus was one of the most beloved members of the faculty. That feeling continued well into the 1990s. Jake loved to tell his "boys" (whatever their gender) about Rabbi Isaac Mayer Wise being assaulted on the pulpit of his congregation in Albany, New York, during the High Holidays in the late 1840s. As he told the story his eyes would sparkle, and a smile would appear on his face as he warned us to be careful. He would say, "I want you all to be successful. I want you all to be significant contributors to our tradition and our history. But treat your congregants properly and never get beat up!"

Rabbi Wise moved to Cincinnati and became the "master builder" of American Reform Judaism, founding the Union for

Reform Judaism, Hebrew Union College, and the Central Conference of American Rabbis. He was, by any definition, very successful and a huge contributor to our tradition and our history. I can't claim any of those successes, but I certainly know that over the course of my career I have aggravated my share of congregants. The last time was within a couple of months of my coming to Temple Emanu-El in Dothan, Alabama. On the way into the sanctuary for services on the morning of *Yom Kippur*, one of the members blocked my path, brushed aside my *tallit*, and grabbed the lapels of my jacket. He pulled my face to within inches of his and said, "You had better learn to do things my way. You had better understand that the way I want it is the way we all want it and we are the ones that matter. You don't." He might have gone on to say more, explaining what it was that he wanted me to do, but I simply said, "And a happy New Year to you as well." I removed his hands from my lapels and walked out onto the *bimah* to conduct the service. I still have no explanation at all for that experience, and we became friends and successful coworkers for our congregation.

In another community, in the Social Hall of a synagogue during an Annual Meeting of the congregation, someone asked a question to which the President asked me to respond. I did so, feeling that I had done a more than adequate job. As I moved toward the back of the room to get a drink, a congregant got out of his seat, stopped me, and in a very loud voice that was heard by everyone in the room said, "Rabbi, you just don't understand that your opinion doesn't matter. You have been our rabbi for two years and probably will be gone within a couple more. We're going to be here for the rest of our lives. Rabbis come and go, but congregations stay and continue. You don't understand that what the Rabbi thinks just doesn't count. The members of the congregation matter. Rabbis don't."

By the time he got to the end of his comments he was shouting, his face was red and all I could think of was how embarrassed I was feeling. Frankly, I had hoped for a long association with that synagogue and my quick reaction was that somehow or other I had blown it. For the rest of the meeting, no one said anything about that confrontation, and I began to believe that everybody agreed with him. When the meeting was over, he came to me in front of a large group of people and offered his apology. He said to me, and to everyone, that he occasionally gets emotionally involved in these kinds of activities and that when he does, it is possible for him to lose his temper and his usual even-handed way of dealing with people. He told me that he was very sorry. I accepted his apology, we shook hands, we hugged, and we became very good friends during my remaining time with that congregation. A few years later he served as its president. Unfortunately, during the second year of his presidency, he died of cancer. He was a man for whom I had the utmost respect and admiration because I discovered that he was big enough to admit a mistake, admit that mistake publicly, get over it very quickly, and move forward to new areas and better relationships.

I haven't always been that lucky. There have been other times when confrontations with congregants were much more dramatic, and unfortunately, much longer lasting. When I arrived

45

at Anshai Emeth in Peoria in 1966, I was told that the religious education program was very poorly structured and that it was a congregational priority to upgrade it significantly. I agreed that it was a priority of mine as well.

It took from July 1966 until the middle of August the following year to create on paper the rules, policies, requirements, and curriculum for the religious and Hebrew schools. All of this was based on a series of goals and objectives which had been determined first. When the work of the committee was completed, everything was submitted to the Board of the congregation for approval. When that approval was granted, the materials were sent to all the families that had children in the religious education program as part of a Parent's Handbook.

On the first Sunday morning of Religious School in September, one father confronted me with these words, "You can't do this. You can't ruin my Sundays." I asked him to sit down with me and to explain to me exactly what was bothering him and what he wanted me to understand. It turned out that he had grown up in that congregation and that his family had been associated with that Jewish community almost from its inception. At the time, he was a sailor and the commodore of the local yacht club. All he wanted was a place where he could drop off his son and daughter on Sunday morning so that he would spend his time with his sailing buddies in the dining room of the yacht club. He wasn't interested in whether his kids learned anything about Judaism. He certainly did not want them to have any homework or any synagogue worship attendance requirements. He just wanted to get rid of his kids on Sunday morning and to otherwise be left alone. When I explained to him that these were not my decisions but rather the work of a congregational committee which had been approved by the Board of Trustees, his comment was, "If you keep this up I'm taking my kids out of Religious School and I will never come back into this building until you leave."

He was true to his word. Nothing that we could do would convince him to bring his children back into our Religious School. Unfortunately for him, we were both members of the Rotary Club which met at noon every Friday. I always sat at a table relatively close to the door, and each week as he walked into the room I stood up and forced him to shake hands with me. It was the only time that we ever saw each other and I could clearly tell that he was very disturbed as I approached him. Five years later, on my last Friday as a member of that Rotary Club, when I shook hands with him I said, "Harry, I'll never bother you again. I'm leaving Peoria in the middle of next week."

I have saved the best and worst story for last. It happened very early in my rabbinic career and it was a public confrontation which I can still visualize very clearly whenever I close my eyes and think about it.

One of my members was a Holocaust refugee who came to America in 1938 when he was a young adult. All of his immediate family died in the camps. He asked an Orthodox rabbi in New

York what he should do to observe *Yahrzeit* for his parents and siblings, as he had no idea of the exact dates of their deaths. He was told to keep *Yom Kippur* as the date and to use the *Yizkor* service on that day to say *Kaddish* for them. He eventually married and fathered a daughter.

He and his family ended up in the community which I served, and he was a successful and respected businessman. Long before my arrival in the community he had assumed the responsibility and the honor of chanting the *Haftarah* reading from Jonah on *Yom Kippur* afternoon as a memorial to his family. During my first High Holidays with that congregation he performed marvelously, and everyone was moved as he reminded those in attendance why he was annually granted this honor. However, my second year there the Ritual Committee met to formalize plans for the holidays. A suggestion was made which led to the calamity that is later described.

There was an elderly gentleman in the congregation who had been a member for sixty years or more. He was very shy and quiet and rarely asked for anything for himself. In the year that I had been the rabbi of the synagogue he had very quietly and politely refused all honors. At that time, however, he was quite ill and many of us thought that he would not live longer than a few more months. At the committee meeting it was suggested that we prevail upon this gentleman to accept an honor that would be very meaningful. The son-in-law of the congregant who always chanted Jonah was a member of the committee, and he suggested to us that he could convince his father-in-law to take another honor for that year so that his elderly friend could have the Jonah reading. When the committee agreed, the son-in-law placed an immediate phone call from the synagogue and much to everyone's surprise and pleasure his father-in-law happily agreed. Within the next day or two I wrote the father-in-law a letter in which I thanked him for his kind and gracious understanding of the situation for those holidays and told him how much I appreciated his willingness to forgo the honor of presenting Jonah to the congregation. I reminded him that I understood how meaningful this was to him, and I suggested that his willingness to permit a dying friend to assume that role was a wonderful example of *mitzvah* and *menschlichkeit*. He called me to thank me for my letter and requested an *Aliyah* for *Yom Kippur* morning as his honor for that year. His request was granted.

This small congregation always brought in an Orthodox gentleman from a larger metropolitan area who could serve as a Cantor for the holidays. He always called the people to the *bimah* for their honors in the traditional way, using their Hebrew names. On the morning of *Yom Kippur,* he called this businessman to the *bimah* for the first *Aliyah* and everything went smoothly as could be hoped.

In the afternoon, when it came time for *Maftir Yonah,* he called for the older, ill gentleman to come to the *bimah* and one of his sons began to help him down the aisle. At that point, our businessman friend jumped up, ran to me on the *bimah,* and started to scream at me with some of the vilest language I had ever heard. Later in the day, one of the women in the congregation commented that she could not believe that this kind of verbal garbage would come from his mouth. Believe it or not, it did! He used every word I had ever heard, and a few combinations that had never occurred to me. After overcoming his shock, the son-in-law came to the *bimah* and escorted his father-in-law out of the building. The rest of the services proceeded smoothly once we had all regained our equilibrium.

The gentleman did not return to the sanctuary for *Yizkor*, and I thought no more of it until five or six minutes into the service when somebody approached the *bimah* and handed me a note. I kept that note for a long time, but in one of my moves it seems to have gotten lost. The note said: "____ is walking up and down the sidewalk in front of the building with a gun in his hand. He is still swearing at you and promises to shoot you." I stopped the service, showed the note to the son-in-law, and asked him to solve the problem. He left the sanctuary and called me on the phone the next day to apologize on behalf of the family. That was the last time that the incident was ever mentioned. While many members of the congregation had heard the original outburst, and a few more had seen him outside with a gun, no one ever said a word about it again, at least as far as I am aware.

By the way, he had *Maftir Yonah* the following year! I might not be Rabbi Isaac Mayer Wise, but I will put my confrontation on the *bimah* up against his any day. His helped to lead him to greatness. Mine only scared me half to death. Rabbi Israel Salanter is quoted as saying, "A Rabbi whose community does not disagree with him is not really a Rabbi, and a Rabbi who fears his community is not really a man."

A Shabbat Walk
and Other Ways of Finding
God

The British philosopher George Whitehead is quoted as having said, "We find God whenever we let him in." In our hectic professional lives, many of us have great difficulty creating opportunities to let God in. We rush from meetings to services to classes to hospital visits to wedding rehearsals to the bereaved family to weddings to funerals. Along the way we prepare students for *B'nai Mitzvah* and Confirmation, while at the same time teaching those who intend to become Jews By Choice. And, if we have the skills and the inclination, we also serve as counselors and religious educators. Occasionally we make time for our families and even provide ourselves with an opportunity to study. Most of us realize that our congregations expect a high degree of professionalism when we function as leaders of worship. We spend a great deal of time in preparing the liturgy, music, readings from *Torah,* and our sermons. If we do our preparations well, the "performance" comes off as effectively as we had hoped, but we realize that it is a performance. There are very little opportunities for us to allow God entrance into our lives. Yet, if we are fortunate, there are many opportunities for us to directly experience God. I have been lucky in that it has happened to me on a number of occasions. I would like to share some with you.

In the summer of 1954, as I was preparing to start my rabbinic studies at the Cincinnati campus of Hebrew Union College-Jewish Institute of Religion, I was required to spend eight weeks in Towanda, Pennsylvania at a program which had just been established for incoming students. Its purpose was to enhance Hebrew knowledge. This was years prior to the Year in Jerusalem Program. We were housed on an estate that had been donated to the college. Almost all my first-year classmates were present along with two or three upperclassmen and Dr. Elias Epstein, the Professor of Hebrew Studies. It was a very intense program and, in retrospect, very beneficial. Even though I was not yet officially a student, I had heard a variety of horror stories describing how difficult the first semester course in Hebrew was and how impossible Weingreen's *Hebrew Grammar* was to master. I am positive that our Towanda experience made things much easier for all of us. The program continued in subsequent years and was eventually moved to the Cincinnati campus. I have not heard a word about it, and I am rather certain that it disappeared when the College-Institute began to require all the students to spend their first year studying in Jerusalem. The Ulpan there is certainly better than studying biblical Hebrew grammar in either Pennsylvania or Ohio.

This will be the third time that I have tried to write the following story. It is very difficult to describe feelings and emotions with written words. It isn't quite as hard when you tell the story to someone. It was part of our regular schedule at Towanda to hold services on *Erev Shabbat* immediately after dinner. If the weather was good, services were held outdoors on the front lawn of the main building of the estate. The estate was at the top of the hill and the lawn sloped downward, to the east, into a narrow valley. A highway and a creek ran north and south through that valley and on the other side the mountains went back up and were covered with trees. We set up our chairs in a semicircle facing east and toward the valley. As services were conducted during the *Erev Shabbat*, the sun was slowly setting behind us. I had noticed that the sunlight striking the hillside directly across from us turned that hill into a strange shade of gold, but beyond thinking of how beautiful it was, it had no special effect on me. At the appropriate time, we all turned to page 71 in the *Union Prayer Book, Newly Revised, Volume I*, and we rose for what was then called the Adoration. As a group, we began to recite:

> Let us adore the ever-living God, and render praise unto Him who spread out the heavens and established the earth, whose glory is revealed in the

heavens above and whose greatness is manifest throughout the world. He is our God, there is none else.

We bow the head in reverence, and worship the King of Kings, the Holy One, praised be He.

I assume that we then sang *Va'anachnu* and sat down, continuing as the person conducting the service read the next paragraph. I cannot remember any of what I have just described except standing up. The next thing I do remember was having Bill Leffler tug at my belt to get me to sit down. We were already passed the halfway mark in the paragraph being read. I know where I was physically, but I cannot describe where I was spiritually and emotionally. I know what happened physically, but not exactly what happened spiritually and emotionally. The only thing that I can attempt to describe is an overwhelming sense of the beauty of my surroundings and an absolute sense of total unity with everything. I felt then, and I feel now, that it was an experience of God, triggered by those specific words in that special environment.

I have already described to you my student rabbi experiences with the *shofar*. As a student rabbi I had the pleasure of sounding the *shofar* for three different student congregations. I think I can say with honesty that I did it well. In the fall of 1959, I was faced with the responsibility of blowing *shofar* for my first "real" congregation and for the first time as an ordained Rabbi. Leaving nothing to chance, I had practiced at least once each day for about a week, and even went to the synagogue building early on *Rosh HaShanah* morning to practice one last time. When I was finished, I placed my *shofar* on the top shelf inside my lectern. It was the practice of the congregation for one of the men to join the rabbi and to chant the names of the various *shofar* sounds. At the appropriate time he appeared at my side and as we finished singing the *b'rachot* I suddenly began to cry uncontrollably. I was totally embarrassed, and at the same time filled with a combination of awe and joy. I could not control my crying, nor could I control my feelings. I don't know how long it took for me to actually stop sobbing, but it certainly felt as if it had taken a very long time. When I was able to, I explained to my congregation exactly what my feelings had been, including my embarrassment. Then I told them that the reason for my crying jag was the fact that I suddenly realized that I was doing something as a real rabbi, not a student, that tens of thousands of other Jews had done over the course of centuries so that tens of millions of other Jews would have the opportunity to fill the *mitzvah* and listen to the sounds of the *shofar*. I said that somehow or other when I blew the *shofar* as a rabbinic student, it wasn't the same. Now that I was an ordained rabbi, I was part of an unbroken chain that had its origin in our biblical past. I tried to convey the sense of heightened spiritual awareness that I had experienced and the feeling of connectedness to our people and our past that had coursed through me. Again, words failed to express the inexpressible. Again, I know what happened, but I cannot adequately describe it to my readers. I have had similar feelings in varying degrees every subsequent *Rosh HaShanah* morning during my career, but never with that intensity. Tears also came to my eyes as I read the first typed draft of these pages, as well as the second and the third.

Early in the summer of 1996 I received a letter from a young woman whose *Bat mitzvah* I had officiated in April 1972. I saw her for the last time when Religious School ended about six weeks later, and I left the community for another congregation. We had no contact between 1972 and 1996. Her letter told me that she had thought about me many times during the intervening years but; however, because her life had been so disturbed and troubled, she had not attempted to make contact. Now, everything had been on an even keel for about four years and she said that she felt that it would be appropriate to write the letter at this time. She referred back to her *Bat mitzvah* and told me, for the first time, exactly how she had felt when her portion of the service had been concluded. The *Torah* was returned to the Ark and I faced her before the open Ark with my hands on her shoulders while I spoke privately to her for a minute or two. She attempted to describe the sense of wellbeing, the feeling of an intense glowing warmth, and a complete lack of awareness of where she was or what was really happening at that moment. She only could say that it was a strong feeling of oneness and a total immersion in what she thought was God.

Her letter continued with the statement that in the few days that followed she was positive that she had experienced God in that moment of time. She said as her life later fell apart, she found herself involved with an unending number of men, alcohol, and a variety of drugs. Reflecting on the day of her *Bat mitzvah* was the only thing that kept her even slightly stable. Now that she had been sober for a few years and actively involved in a 12-step program, she knows quite clearly that those few moments in her life linked her forever with her Higher Power. A few months after her letter, she arranged to drive through Dothan on her way back to her home in southern Florida. We spent a few very precious hours together talking about her *Bat mitzvah*, the subsequent terrors in her life, and the pleasures and the pride of her continued recovery.

When I arrived at Beth Israel Congregation in Florence, South Carolina, during the summer of 1984, I met a woman who was slightly older than me and had been very active in the congregation for many years. I quickly learned that she had been raised in one of the larger cities on the east coast in a strictly Orthodox congregation. She had received a very minimal Jewish education and had obviously never had the opportunity to assume any type of leadership role in her home congregation, certainly not in a participating way in any service. She married a man whose family lived in a small community just outside of Florence. They moved there so that he could take over the family store. Before too long, they had children and as she brought them to the synagogue building for education purposes, she became more and more involved. She eventually chaired a variety of congregational committees, became a member of the Board of Trustees, and when I arrived she was serving as the elected secretary. I make it a practice in all my congregations to ask two members of the Board to sit with me on the *bimah* during every service and to assist by opening and closing the Ark, dressing and undressing the *Torah,* and so forth. She told me that one of my predecessors had done something similar. On one Friday night, she was one of those sitting on the *bimah* in chairs flanking the Ark. After the rabbi had read from the *Torah,* he rolled it closed and tied it together. He then picked it up from the lectern and put it in her lap for her to hold while it was being dressed. As she told me this story, her exact words were, "I felt that I had God in my arms."

A few years later she took the adult education *Introduction to Hebrew Reading* course which I offered and found that she learned that primary skill quite easily. She then determined to become an adult *Bat mitzvah.* She put her whole mind and all her energy into that endeavor and soon we were making specific plans for her participation as a *Torah* reader, *Haftarah* reader, and speech maker. When I work with children for their *Bar* or *Bat mitzvah,* I never permit them to have parental assistance in writing their short talk. I strongly feel that it needs to be the teenager's work exclusively and that the parents need the experience of hearing something totally fresh on the occasion of their child's *Bar* or *Bat mitzvah.* Goodness knows that they help the kids learn and rehearse everything else.

This woman was also told to write her adult *Bat mitzvah* talk without my assistance so that I would have the opportunity to hear something that *Erev Shabbat* in which I had not been personally and professionally involved. In her talk she referred to her upbringing and retold the story of having the *Torah* placed into her arms for the first time. She went on to comment that she felt exactly the same way when I took the *Torah* out of the Ark that night and handed it to her for her to carry around the sanctuary for *Hakafah*. She spent a great deal of time attempting to explain her feelings to those in attendance so that they might understand how much this occasion meant to her. She reflected on her youth as an Orthodox Jew and her adult involvement as a member of a Reform congregation. She tried to help people understand how fortunate she felt they were to have had lifelong Reform Jewish opportunities and experiences.

A "*Shabbat* Walk" is mentioned in the title of this chapter. Furthermore, this chapter describes an experience which I had during the recitation of the "Adoration" during the summer of 1954 in Towanda, Pennsylvania. As I began to work with MSTY in a camp setting, it occurred to me that maybe I could recreate that Towanda experience for the kids who were participating in our camp conclaves. I tried it out, and it worked fairly well. It was further developed as an exercise of trying to help kids find God during my summers at OSRUI. What I will describe for you is more or less its final form. I will also tell you that it works.

I always made sure that cabin counselors knew that I would be available to them and to their campers for a *Shabbat* Walk any Friday night that they wanted it. It would be outside, and it would require their kids to sit or lie on the ground, so the weather had to cooperate. If a cabin or two chose to participate, the counselors were told to bring their kids to a certain spot after evening program activities had ended. The campers were not permitted to carry anything in their hands including flashlights, sweaters, or jackets. If campers wanted to bring those items, they had to be worn. I met the kids at the appointed time and place and told them that I had only two requirements for what I thought would be a very special activity. In the first place, I asked them to follow my instructions as quickly and exactly. Secondly, I told them that no one, under any circumstances, was to talk unless it was an emergency. I suggested that if they could not follow these two strict but simple rules, they would have the option of returning to their cabin or tent.

When we were ready, I led the kids away from camp into an area where there was no ambient light and it was as dark as possible. We walked very slowly in single file and after a while I asked them to stop. I said, "Please stand perfectly still and put all of your energy into listening. Listen as carefully and as hard as you can for even the smallest sounds." I knew that they would be able to hear a dog barking in the distance, the wind rustling the leaves at their feet, the sound of a frog, the noise made by insects, and occasionally the sound of some small animal moving through the field.

After a rather long pause, I asked them to continue following me and we walked for another few minutes. Then, I asked them to stop and this time to try to turn their skin into an organ of perception. I asked them to continue to try to hear, but at the same time to use their skin to feel. Again, I knew that they would feel either the breeze or the wind on their faces or on their arms. I knew that some would feel the weeds and the bushes against their legs.

And again, after an appropriate pause, we moved on and walked farther away from the camp and more deeply into the darkness. When we stopped the third time, I asked them to try to continue to hear and to attempt to continue to feel. I asked them to look up toward the sky and to experience whatever they saw there. I knew that on most summer nights in Wisconsin the stars were numerous and bright and so close that they appeared to be touchable. We then walked on a little farther and when we stopped, I asked everybody to lie down on their back without talking and without their body being in contact with anybody else's. I said to them, "Once you are in position, please close your eyes." After waiting for a suitable time for them to adjust to their new posture and circumstances, I reminded them to keep their eyes closed and I began to talk:

> It is *Erev Shabbat* and we have walked together for quite a while. We have experienced together our hearing, our sense of touch, and the nighttime sky with our eyes. Now, I am going to recite some words for you. They are words that you all know by heart. They are words that you recited earlier this evening. Please remember to keep your eyes closed. Let us adore the ever Living God, and render praise unto Him who spread out the Heavens and established the earth, whose glory is revealed in the Heavens above and whose greatness is manifest throughout the world. He is our God, there is none else.

(There was a short pause.) Now, would you please recite those words with me:

Now, it is time for you to open your eyes to look above at the Heavens, to feel the earth under your back, and to remember all that we have experienced so far. (I was silent for at least five to ten minutes.)

I think that it would be very beneficial if we recited those words together one more time.

After another pause of two or three minutes I reminded the campers that their obligation was to remain quiet. I told them that they could now stand up and get back in line. I told them that there would be no talking as we slowly made our way back to camp, but it would be OK to walk side by side and hold hands if they wanted to.

The walk back to camp usually took three or four minutes because we would not stop. However, I did walk as slowly as possible. The whole experience lasted about 40-45 minutes.

As we came closer to camp, we became more aware of lights in the various buildings and the lights on poles which provided illumination for the grounds. As we came out of the field and onto the grass that had been mowed as part of the camp lawn, I thanked the kids for inviting me to lead them on the *Shabbat* Walk and I told them that I appreciated their cooperation and now they were free to talk. Time and time again campers told me that it had been one of the most moving experiences of their lives. Many had tears in their eyes. Campers who are now my colleagues remind me that they participated in that experience when they were young kids and that it made a lasting impression on them.

We all have the ability to lead each other to valuable spiritual and religious experiences. We don't try it often enough. I wish that I could figure out a way to take the adults in my congregation on a *Shabbat* Walk like the one described above. It still works!

Taking Advantage: Good and Bad

One day in the early 1970s I was driving along the Pennsylvania turnpike and noticed the flashing lights of a police car approaching rapidly behind me. Along with everyone else, I was driving slightly over the speed limit and felt that moment of apprehension and fear. The police car had moved into the left-hand lane and was about to pass me when it slowed down and fell into line behind me, so I moved to the shoulder of the road and parked my car. A state trooper approached my window and told me that he had noticed the bumper sticker on the rear which said, "clergy." He asked me if I would be willing to follow him about ten miles up the road to the scene of an accident and minister to the people who were the injured survivors. Of course, I agreed. For the first time in my life, I followed the flashing lights rather than watch them in the rear-view mirror. We pulled into the median and he introduced me very quickly to the other officers on the scene, one of whom escorted me to a group of people sitting or lying on the grass. Their car had been hit from behind and had rolled in the median. Thankfully, they were all wearing seatbelts and while the injuries were not life threatening, they were severely hurt and extremely emotional. I talked to them individually, giving them assurances that paramedics were on the way. I prayed with them and offered what assistance I could until they were removed from the scene in ambulances.

When I returned from my trip, I found a letter waiting for me from the officer in charge of the State Patrol district thanking me for my cooperation and assistance to keep the family calm and composed until further help arrived. A couple of weeks later, I received a letter from the family indicating that they were all at home and well on the way to recovery and, again, offering thanks for my kindnesses. Obviously, on that occasion the clergy sign on the car was beneficial.

On another occasion maybe eight to ten years earlier, my wife took the children downtown and pulled into a parking space on the street. As she was fumbling in her purse for the change for the parking meter, one of my kids said to her, "Why don't you just flip down the clergy sign on the sun visor the way Daddy does?" She put the appropriate money in the meter, and in a laughing sort of way told me the story later in the day. It was quite clear to me that I had been setting a totally improper example for my children and that I had been teaching them to take advantage of my particular circumstances. You may be certain that I never used the word "clergy" in that way again.

At about the same time, I owned a red MG-A convertible. During the intense Wisconsin winter, that little sports car never got much of a workout. One afternoon in the spring, I went out into the more rural part of the county and drove it rather rapidly, in low gears, with very high RPM, along a couple of county roads trying to get the engine very hot and burn out some of the accumulated carbon. A sheriff's deputy pulled me over, walked up to the car and asked what I was doing. I told him. He told me to follow him. We turned around and drove back inside the city limits and I parked as he pulled over to the curb. He then walked back to my car and said, "Rabbi, race your little car and burn out the carbon in the city. Just don't do it in my county." Again, I was wrong. Again, my status as a clergy person came to my rescue. Again, I ended up feeling lousy.

In a course that Sylvan Schwartzman taught to rabbinic students and their wives at HUC in Cincinnati during the final semester immediately prior to ordination, he attempted to give us some insight into what he called the practical rabbinate. I still have detailed notes on those discussions. Among them was the suggestion that as we came into a new community, we should automatically make introductory visits to the mayor, the head elected official in the county, the city and/or county executive if there was one, and to the police chief and the fire chief. Additionally, he suggested that we talk to the members of our congregation to find out which of the service Clubs, usually either

Rotary or Kiwanis, was the most prestigious in town. Sylvan suggested that we attempt to find a congregant who would sponsor us for membership in whichever of the clubs we selected. I moved to Battle Creek, Michigan in July 1959. By January of 1960, I was a member of the Rotary Club. I remained a Rotarian through October of 1994, with only a few years of nonparticipation. These experiences were very valuable to me, just as were his suggestions that I introduce myself to the leadership of the various communities in which I served.

There have been many times throughout my career when it was quite beneficial to me or to my synagogue to be able to pick up the phone and call one of the community leaders that I had met to obtain an answer to a question, ask for a favor, or simply to discuss an issue that was of concern. With rare exception, the people that I met in this way have proven to be extraordinarily helpful.

In one instance, we had a series of minor vandalism incidents at the synagogue building. It was very easy to place a phone call directly to the police chief and quickly increase the number of police patrols around the building. The vandalism ceased immediately and never recurred. I am confident that because I had gone to introduce myself to the police chief and had met him on several other occasions at Rotary meetings, it made it quite easy for him to accommodate the synagogue's needs in the work schedule of his department.

On many occasions when I visited congregants in the hospital, I also met their attending physician. I was able to discuss the situation and circumstances with the doctor in such a way as to help the physician understand some of the family's concerns. At the same time, I was able to assure family members that their loved one was getting along as well as could be expected under the circumstances. Any time that the Rabbi can be an intermediary between helping professionals and family members, it can be of significant benefit to both. My participation in Rotary made that an easy opportunity for me quite frequently.

If you turn that coin over, it works just as well. There are two occasions that come to my mind immediately when I was called by a physician who knew me from Rotary and asked me to talk to family members of a patient because the doctor was concerned that they were not completely understanding the medical circumstances. On both occasions, the doctor suggested that I meet him in the patient's room the next morning as rounds were being made, and I arranged to bring members of the family with me. These interventions were highly successful, at least in terms of the way family members felt about the health circumstances of their loved ones. They came away from those relatively brief discussions with a much clearer understanding of what was happening, why, and what the prognosis may have been.

I remember a member of Rotary asking if he could sit with me at a Monday noon meeting of the Club. He was very concerned about something that had been said about Jews and Judaism in the Sunday School class which he had attended the day before at his church. When we talked about it, it was clear that the teacher's comments were highly anti-Semitic and very inaccurate. I casually knew the pastor of the church through our mutual involvement of one of the local clergy groups. I thought him to be a very reasonable person. At my suggestion, my fellow Rotarian made an appointment for himself and for me to visit with the clergyman the following day. When the incident in Sunday morning's class was described to the minister, he was nowhere near as concerned about it as I was. However, as our conversation continued, he began to understand my point of view and why his own church member and I reacted as we did. After about an hour of discussion, he picked up the phone and called the Sunday School teacher and made it very clear that he was upset by what had been said in class on Sunday. Furthermore, he indicated to the teacher that he had invited me to speak in that classroom the following Sunday morning. That involved a great deal of rearranging of my own calendar and my own involvement with our Religious School, but it turned out to be well worth it. I discovered that many of the other students were similarly disturbed by the teacher's comments but didn't know what to do about it. None of them had ever met me previously and none had thought of the possibility of calling me.

The end result was that I spent four consecutive Sunday mornings with that particular class and delivered the sermon at the main service in that church on the fifth Sunday. In all five appearances, I spoke about the relationship of Judaism and Christianity and how the church was an outgrowth of the synagogue. I emphasized that while there are very fundamental variances in our primary theology's ideas, we shared a great deal in common. I am convinced that my relationship with the one church member through Rotary gave me the opportunity to have a significant impact on many members' lives within an important church in our community. Without Rotary, it probably never would have happened.

My involvement with clergy groups in the various communities that I served was quite pleasant most of the time, yet very strange in my later years. Beginning in Battle Creek and continuing through Topeka, Kansas in the summer of 1984, I was always welcomed into the community that I served by my Christian colleagues and invited to be a part of the basic ministerial or clergy association. In many of those towns I became an officer of the group and three different times I was elected president. I never had any difficulty being accepted.

However, there were some occasions when vocabulary presented problems. I don't think that it is proper to use exclusive language in mixed groups. For example, in mixed religious groups the words used to describe a place of worship should be "church and synagogue" or "congregation" instead of the simple word "church." Similarly, the word "clergy" should be used to replace "minister" or "pastor." Inclusive language is always best. Whenever I ran up against this problem in years past, a simple word or two of explanation was enough to change language behavior and the attempt at a solution never led to any difficulties.

However, during the time I wrote this book I noticed a very significant change. It may have had to do with the times that we lived in, or the fact that in the summer of 1984 I moved to the bible belt of Dixie. During that time it was very difficult to get people to understand my desire for inclusive language. Nonetheless, I am not a minister or pastor and the institution that I served was not a church. If my Christian colleagues wanted me to continue to participate in their group, they needed to be sufficiently welcoming to use language which included me rather than excluded me.

During this time I also requested that the opening prayer for the brief liturgy at the meetings be changed so that it included the feelings and attitudes of all of those in attendance, not just the Christians. That likewise had never presented a problem until I moved to the bible belt of Dixie. After all, Jews and Christians alike can recite a Psalm without offending anybody's religious sensibilities. We can all comfortably pray without saying that our prayers are directed to God through Jesus.

At least that's what I thought until I moved south. In Florence, South Carolina, there were four clergy groups. Two were white and two were black. One of each race might have been called the mainline congregations (and that's the group to which I was invited) while the other was best described as fundamentalists, Pentecostal, or charismatic. Efforts were repeatedly made to find ways to bridge the gap between these four groups, but to no avail. Interestingly, none of the clergy who served the large churches in Florence participated in any of the four clergy groups. We tried to solve that problem as well by visiting some of these pastors in their offices, having lunch with them, and on occasion inviting them to present their programs to our association. They were always polite they always spoke nicely to us, they accepted our invitations to present their programs, but they never joined us.

In Dothan, I was invited to attend my first group meeting within three or four weeks after arriving in the community by a pastor of a church affiliated with Presbyterian-USA. He and the minister of an Evangelical Lutheran Church in America picked me up and took me to the meeting. From September to May in my first year I had put up with the highly Christian atmosphere of the opening prayer and the primary content of the meeting. Over the summer, I wrote a letter to the incoming president that asked him to be sensitive to these issues and made some suggestions for ways in which additional non-Christian programming could be accomplished. He never replied, but at the very first meeting he introduced a member of the group to deliver the opening prayer which contained phrases such as, "We all are believers in Christ, and we all have accepted Jesus into our lives." The entire prayer lasted for three or four minutes, was in the plural, and almost every sentence referenced Christ or Jesus. When it was over, I raised my hand and asked the president and the group whether I was welcomed to be a member of that association of clergy. I was asked why I had raised the question and I responded by referring to the opening prayer. I indicated that the theology of the prayer did not include me and that I was offended by the use of the plural pronoun, "we." That provided the opportunity for some discussion and while I was supported by the Presbyterian and the Lutheran minister who had brought me to my very first meeting, no one else in the group seemed to understand what the three of us were talking about.

In our private conversations we three decided to attend the October meeting in 1996 to see what, if anything, would develop. Once again, we were made to feel very uncomfortable and none of us returned to a meeting. I called the two clergy members during the summer of 1997 as I was writing this book to find out if anybody from the clergy association had contacted them to discover why these two very active members were no longer participants. Neither received a phone call or letter, and obviously nobody got in touch with me to find out why I was no longer a participant. I guess our request was simply too difficult for people with very narrow or parochial religious outlooks to either understand or to accommodate.

Nonetheless, my involvement in Rotary, the clergy associations in the various communities which I have served, and my visits to the civic leadership in the towns of which I served opened many doors for me. Because of this involvement, I have been asked on numerous occasions to join Human Relations Commissions, committees, boards of various United Ways, and numerous other civic boards. My guess is that little of that would have been possible if I had not taken Sylvan Schwartzman's advice. Furthermore, I feel that if we, as Rabbis, expect our lay people to be involved in any of the activities which comes under the broad heading of *Tikkun Olam*, we then need to serve as role models. As Rabbis, we need to be involved in the good works of the communities which we serve to the very best of our abilities and to the fullest extent of our available time and resources. But, more of that in later chapters. This one is already too serious!

Sermons and Other Sentient Sayings

When we were students at HUC in Cincinnati, one of the classes that we took dealt with a combination of *Midrash* and what the professor named Dr. Israel Bettan called, "the casual speech." By that he meant the talks that we gave at life cycle ceremonies which were generally considerably shorter than sermons. He insisted that every such talk had to have some very specific Judaic content and that content should always be derived from one of our texts. Because of his area of scholarship, he generally suggested that it be *Midrash*.

In one particular class we ran through a series of *Midrashim*, and he indicated how they could be used on various occasions such as weddings, funerals, or a *Brit Milah* (Jewish religious circumcision). He then went on to say that the most important thing we needed to remember was that every talk at a funeral had to praise the deceased. He said something like, "It is very necessary that you always say something nice about the dead, because you really are attempting to make the surviving family feel better. That is your most important task." One of the students interrupted and said, "But, Dr., what if the guy we are burying was an absolute gold-plated nogoodnik?" Dr. Bettan responded by saying, "At the very least, say that he smiled at his mother and build on that."

At that time in my life I had never even attended a funeral, much less conducted one. Nonetheless, the comment must have had a very deep impression on me because I have used it at every one of the hundreds of funerals I have conducted. Furthermore, I believe that it really ties in beautifully with the concept that our tradition teaches, "The memory of the righteous is a blessing." It has become obvious to me over the years that memory is selective. No matter how poorly a child may have been treated by his or her parent, after death that child begins to remember the pleasant, happy, and wonderful experiences that involved the parent. The bad things seem to disappear. As Rabbis, if we emphasize the good aspects of the individual in our eulogy, it assists the family as they process the memories of their loved ones.

The very first funeral I conducted was in Portsmouth, Ohio, during my last year at HUC. I got a phone call at about 9:00 on a Monday night from a congregant and was told that his sister had died earlier in the evening. Her body was being brought to

Portsmouth by train and was scheduled to arrive mid-morning the following day. I was asked if I would be available to conduct a funeral at 1:30 the next afternoon. "Of course," I responded affirmatively and was immediately invited to join the family for lunch at their home. When the phone call was completed I called my mentor, Sylvan Schwartzman, and basically gave a *Shrie Gevalt*. Remember, I had never attended a funeral and now I was expected to conduct my first one. Sylvan led me through my *Rabbi's Manual*, page by page, and gave me some indication of the things that I needed to do. He asked me if I had any idea what I might say the following day at the funeral. I told him that I hadn't thought about it yet, but I knew that I still had my notes from Dr. Bettan's class and so it shouldn't be particularly difficult to find something appropriate. He asked me if I was going to have an opportunity to see the family before the funeral and I told him about lunch. His comment was very simple. "Listen carefully. Repeat the good things that they say."

I guess that the funeral was successful, if that word is appropriate. The family certainly seemed pleased and satisfied and they felt that the remarks which I made about their sister and mother summed up her life in a way that was meaningful to them. All I had done was follow Bettan's and Schwartzman's advice.

At this point, I think it is important for me to say that I always speak extemporaneously. I delivered the required two sermons on *Shabbat* morning in the chapel at HUC, one in my fourth year and one in my fifth, both of which had been written out fully. I don't know how it works now, but in those days we were required to submit a first draft of the sermon to a faculty member approximately ten days in advance. I did this during my fifth year and he suggested that I remove one paragraph and substitute it for a different idea. I rewrote the sermon as per his suggestion and submitted it for his approval. It was promptly received. I then took the sermon to one of the college's secretaries who typed it on a stencil, mimeographed it, and had enough copies available at the back of the chapel on Saturday morning for everyone present to take one if desired. All students and faculty where invited to a session the following Monday to analyze the sermon. We began with Dr. Lowell McCoy, an ordained Methodist minister (and an excellent third baseman) who was the speech professor. He played back portions of the tape and shared with me and everyone else who was present what he felt had gone well and what had not.

Then, the faculty member who oversaw the writing of the sermon began his critique. He started out by telling me that the sermon was generally very good, but it had one significant flaw. He suggested that a paragraph was inappropriate and recommended a different idea in its place. Sure enough, he criticized the paragraph that I had inserted at his suggestion and recommended my original idea as the one that should have replaced it. Unfortunately, my big mouth took over. I pointed out to him and everybody else that I had the original draft of the sermon in my briefcase and that he was the one who had originally suggested that the idea and paragraph be removed. I suggested that he was a more than dishonest phony and I was no longer interested in any kind of discourse with him. I immediately left the room and have no idea what transpired afterwards.

The experience of attempting to communicate with a congregation from a written text made me very uncomfortable. In Portsmouth, I began to experiment with sermons that had not been previously written out. I always make certain that I knew weeks in advance what I would talk about and generally what ideas I wished to communicate. Once that had been determined, I structured the sermon and developed some of the wording in my head as I drove my car, took a shower, or did other mindless kinds of activities. I also learned how to communicate to the congregation with eye contact and facial expressions. I have been told very frequently that I am an excellent preacher and that my sermons are generally well worth hearing. That doesn't mean that some of them haven't been stinkers. They have, most assuredly.

This type of preaching requires a very strict sense of discipline in order to be successful. Over the course of time, I managed to achieve this by listing all my sermon titles in the Bulletin along with a two or three sentence description of what it was that I intended to say. Since I chose to spend most of my career in small congregations, it meant that I functioned in a setting where the Bulletin was published monthly. I attempted to remember to turn in the worship schedule, including the list of sermons, about ten days to two weeks before the Bulletin was printed. That generally meant that I had already made up my mind about the first sermon of the month anywhere from two to three weeks in advance of the time that it was delivered. In the same way, if there were five weekends in the month, I focused on a sermon seven or eight weeks away. That certainly provided an adequate opportunity for research, thought, and preparation even when the text of the sermon was not fully written out.

With the same sense of discipline, I always went into the sanctuary on Friday morning to rehearse the complete service that I was going to conduct that evening. I read the *siddur* out loud. I read the *Torah* and *Haftarah* portions out loud. If I could, in a congregation where I lead the singing, I rehearsed that as well. Please remember that extemporaneous does not equal unprepared.

Over the course of a long rabbinate, there obviously were times when I did not have the opportunity to prepare myself for a service in accordance with the standard that I set. This might have been the result of illness, personal pressure, or something unforeseen occurring within the congregation. During these situations, even though the title and outline of the sermon had been printed in the Bulletin, I always told my congregation on *Erev Shabbat* that I was not prepared for the published sermon and did something else in its place. I would instead lead a discussion on a current topic which I thought was beneficial or conducted an, "Ask the Rabbi" session or something similar. Over the course of the years I developed too much respect for my congregants and profession to attempt something as important as a sermon when I was not ready. I don't think that *Erev Shabbat* is the time for a snow job. That is a lesson I learned in my early teen years from the senior rabbi of my home congregation, Rabbi Barnett R. Brickner. I very clearly remember a Friday evening when he came to the lectern at the time set aside for his sermon and with a very nasally voice told us that he had been ill during the week and simply had not had the opportunity to adequately prepare to deliver a sermon. He suggested instead that members of the congregation ask him questions which he would do his best to answer. I remember it as a very interesting evening.

Now, I would like to share with you some excerpts from some of the sermons that I have delivered over the course of my career. Except for the first, all have been transcribed from the tape because they were delivered extemporaneously. The first one entitled, *Was It a Happy Birthday, George?* is a sermon dialogue for Brotherhood Week. It was delivered at Temple Beth El in Battle Creek, Michigan on February 23, 1962. Because it was a dialogue between me and the offstage voice of George Washington, it had to be fully scripted. It was subsequently printed by an anonymous donor and distributed to all the members of the congregation. What follows are some excerpts:

> **Rabbi:** I wonder if I might ask you how you feel about this special week which we always celebrate at the time of your birthday. Would you care to tell me your ideas about Brotherhood Week?

> **GW:** This is another one of the areas which gives me cause for some concern. As I look down

on the present American scene, it is important that each citizen have knowledge of, and information about, the religious beliefs, attitudes, and practices of those other faiths. But is it really necessary to set a special week aside, dedicated to the ideal of brotherhood? I question the need for the whole program. Didn't we settle all this once-and-for-all when we laid the foundation of this country? Didn't we say, "... that *all* men are created *equal...* "?

Rabbi: We might say that we have not attempted to read between the lines, that we have not made the connections between being created, God the Creator and Father, and the implied idea of the brotherhood of man.

GW: I can't understand that. It was so obvious at the time. You know, Jefferson expressed it very clearly, he made the connections which you mentioned when he said, "The God who gave us life, gave us liberty at the same time."

The dialogue continued in a similar way for a few more minutes and then it continues as follows:

GW: What was it that president Kennedy said regarding Brotherhood Week? I can't seem to remember exactly.

Rabbi: His statement reads, "The question for our time is not whether all men are brothers. That question has been answered by the God who placed us on this earth together. The question is whether we have the strength and the will to make the brotherhood of man the guiding principle of our daily lives."

GW: Yes, that's the one. A contemporary of mine said a similar thing about our individual responsibility and about our obligation. Thomas Paine expressed it this way, "Those who expect to reap the blessings of freedom must, like men, undergo the fatigues of supporting it."

Rabbi: Possibly you have put your finger on the basis of our problem. I believe that you have helped me understand and appreciate more fully some of the difficulty I have encountered in attempting to direct so much of my time and effort to finding a solution to these manifold problems. There is effort, there is work, there will be fatigue involved in this endeavor. And seemingly, people are not willing to make this kind of sacrifice. It appears as if most do not care enough to help, yet they would be the first to cry out if any of their freedoms were threatened. One becomes rather discouraged quite quickly.

That sermonic dialogue continued for another couple of pages. I have used it twice subsequently, once a few years later in Kenosha, Wisconsin, and then in the late 1960s in Peoria, Illinois. By the way, the sensitive reader will clearly understand that the dialogue was not gender inclusive. I have chosen not to edit these sermons at all and I offer no apology for the fact that some of them were delivered before my own sensitivity to gender issues was well developed.

The next sermon that I pulled from my files was from 1964 and dealt with social action issues. I will refer to it when I address that topic in the next chapter.

This sermon came from Temple Beth Shalom in Topeka, Kansas. It was delivered on Friday evening, March 16, 1984, immediately after I returned from Cincinnati where I had received my Honorary Doctor of Divinity after completing 25 years in the Reform Rabbinate. After my ordination, I visited the college in 1960 when HUC-JIR presented an honorary degree to the poet Robert Frost. I visited Cincinnati again in the middle 1970s when I took my daughter Debi to visit the University of Cincinnati and HUC where she was planning to enroll to pursue her undergraduate degree in Judaic studies. As I have indicated to you previously, I was at Plum Street Temple in Cincinnati in June 1982 for the ordination of Gary Zola. Those were the only visits that I made to HUC between the time of my ordination and my honorary DD 25 years later. Again, edited from the transcription from the tape, here are some of the things that I said:

I want to tell you a little bit of some of the things that I saw at the college in June of 1982, and when I was there for ordination this past Wednesday. I want to tell you about them, because I think that some of the changes that have taken place at the College are very important, not because Hebrew Union College trains Reform rabbis, but rather because Hebrew Union College mirrors and reflects Reform Judaism. I think that it is important for you to understand what I just said. The college mirrors the reality of what goes on in our congregations. The college does not create it. The college took me as I was and gave me the opportunity to grow and to develop and to change. But unless they are much more subtle than I can give them credit for, they didn't force that growth and that development into any particular channels. So, the changes that I see at the college are changes that were brought to the college by the students and the faculty rather than imposed on the students and faculty.

I then spent some time reflecting on what I had observed as I walked through the halls and noticed the sequential pictures of each year's group of ordainees. I commented specifically on a couple of significant changes. Among the things that I noticed and commented on were the fact that in the 1970s most of the male students were bearded, while only one of the 19 with whom I was ordained wore a beard. Almost every student, male and female, wore a *tallit* and a *kipah*. I then continued with these remarks:

> Now I think that those two things together say something about Reform Judaism. The fact remains that in a sense, we as Reform Jews have agreed that it is OK to be distinctly Jewish. That it is OK to have a beard and maybe look rabbinic. That it is OK to dress a little differently in the synagogue, to wear a *tallit* and *kipah*. It is all right for those kinds of distinctly Jewish behaviors to be part of our Jewish tradition now. I don't think it would have been all right in the 1950s. There was a student at the college a year or two ahead of me, and he always wore a *kipah* all the time. He wore it when he tried to play baseball with us, he wore it in class, he wore it when we would go down to the corner for a beer. When he wanted to wear it as he conducted services in the chapel at Hebrew Union College, he was hassled by some of the members of the faculty in the 1950s. The college at that time reflected, in a sense, the orthodoxy of Reform. The unwritten *Halachah*, the unwritten religious law, was that if you went into a Reform Temple, you did it with your head uncovered. Thankfully, we've changed.

I then spoke about the fact that women were students at Hebrew Union College, that Sally Priesand had been ordained in

1972, and that I had heard her deliver the ordination address in 1982 on the tenth anniversary of her ordination. About 35% to 40% of the students in the ordination pictures from 1972 through 1983 were women. Then I continued with these words:

> Please understand what I said. The college has always been open to women. Society wasn't ready. Our congregations weren't ready. The signals that we were giving to our young women, to our students in our religious schools, were all masculine signals. So, none chose to make the attempt. In the 1960s, some began to do that. In the 1960s society, Reform Judaism had changed enough so that the college as the mirror of our congregations began to have women in its classes. It began to ordain women as rabbis.

I then moved on to something else:

> When I was a student at the college, the chapel looked like a typical synagogue of its time. Above the Ark and behind it was a choir loft, there was a wall across the front of the *bimah*, very clearly separating the pulpit from the pew. Steps were on one side and the other, very clearly dividing that one area from the other. The chapel was stark.

> The chapel had been completely remodeled and renovated somewhere between 1960 and 1984.

The entire *bimah* had been removed. Now it is a platform that is completely open. There is just one simple step up from the floor of the sanctuary to the *bimah*. Even more importantly than that, the lectern that used to be big and forbidding and, in the middle, now is forward and off to one side. The person that is conducting the service, the person that is preaching, is surrounded by the congregation, there are people sitting on the sides. And it is very, very close. The outstanding feature of the present chapel at HUC is the Ark from the 1700s, off to one side and carved out of wood. It originally had been part of an old wooden Polish synagogue. For years and years and years that Ark had been on display in the Hebrew Union College Museum. It was an artifact. Somebody had the good sense to take an artifact, a relic, and turn it again into something that was once again alive and living. Here is the beautiful, modem sanctuary with that very, very old Ark. And it fits so well because we have learned, you and I as Reform Jews, that we cannot give up our past. We have learned that we need to be true to it, in our own way to be sure, but we need to be true to our roots.

I concluded with this paragraph:

Hebrew Union College has come a long way in 25 years. When I attended ordination in 1982 after having attended my previous one in 1959, I literally felt that I was in the wrong building. The change was so dramatic. Then, I came to understand it a little. And when I experienced some more of it this past Wednesday, I understood it even better. There are some who sometimes suggest that change makes us uncomfortable. I can only tell you that this change made me feel very proud.

The next sermon was delivered exactly two weeks later to the same congregation and was a series of personal reflections on my 25 years in the rabbinate. You have already read a good number of the stories I told the congregation that night in this book. Near the end of the sermon, I reflected about interreligious cooperation and understanding. I said the following:

I learned so much from being forced to involve myself in interreligious affairs, to shed whatever it was, fear, hesitancy, distress that held me back. I have learned that the pluralism that is part of the makeup of the United States really does work. It really does if you will give it a chance. It is not a melting pot, it's a symphony or it is a mosaic. The red doesn't lose its ability to be red when it is put on a piece of canvas next to some blue. The red stays red and the blue stays blue. The red maintains its redness and the blue maintains its blueness. The violin in the orchestra remains and is always a violin and the flute in the orchestra is always a flute. When they join, they add, and they blend. One doesn't override the other, one doesn't take away from the other. They don't move and melt together somehow and lose their individuality. It is through that pluralism, that adding together of difference, that we get the painting or the symphony or the society in which we live.

The next sermon that I want to quote for you was delivered at Temple Beth Israel in Florence, South Carolina on Friday evening, September 20, 1985. That night was the beginning of *Shabbat Shuvah*. The sermon was entitled: "A Personal Act of Repentance: My Refusal to Recite the Pledge of Allegiance." After some introductory remarks, the sermon continued:

It was sometime during the Fall of 1967. I was a Rabbi in Peoria, Illinois. I was a member of the Peoria Human Relations Commission, and in that capacity, I was asked to be one of two keynote speakers at a daylong human rights and civil rights workshop held in the community under the auspices of city government. The mayor was the other keynote speaker.

We were on the stage of one of the high schools, and the person who chaired the meeting said, "Let us begin by reciting the Pledge of Allegiance to the flag." Everyone on the stage and everyone in the audience, myself included, turned to face the flag. We all put our hands over our hearts, and we all began to speak. We said those words that are so well known.

The mayor spoke first, and in his remarks, he said something to the effect that if he had been black rather than white, the city hall of Peoria would have been burned down long ago. As the mayor, he was incensed that the community had made such little progress by 1967, twelve years after Rosa Parks had refused to move to the back of the bus. Then it was my turn.

I said to those folks, that I had just that day, within just a few minutes, experienced one of the most difficult times of my life. I told them that I had been asked to stand there in public, in front of them, with my hand over my heart, to recite the Pledge of Allegiance to the flag. I told them I did it, but that I would never do it again.

I said to them, I won't do it because it isn't true. I have no problem with pledging my allegiance to the United States of America. I have no problem with pledging my allegiance to its flag. That isn't the part that bothers me. What bothers me is the pious platitude that comes next. The plain, simple, untruth that states clearly that we are one nation under God, with liberty and justice for all. I said to my audience that morning, maybe if you are middle class and white the Pledge of Allegiance is true. But if you are black in Peoria or if you are Hispanic in Peoria, or if you are Native American in Peoria, those words ring hollow. The incident passed, the day went off without a hitch and that was the end of that until December of 1970.

Two things happened in December of 1970. One was that a group of black, young people began to attend meetings of the Peoria City Council and refused to stand up at the beginning of the meeting when the Pledge of Allegiance was recited. In a very quiet way, these young people were carrying their protest into City Hall. The City Hall that I remind you that the mayor said would have burned if he had been black. Their protest was very quiet by comparison and yet it raised a huge furor in town because these young blacks, high school and college students, refused to recite the pledge. At the same time, in an issue of Look Magazine, dated December 1, 1970, an article was published entitled, "Do We Need A New Pledge of Allegiance?" The author's answer was a resounding yes. "Yes, We Do," he said, and he authored one.

Now, from the time I first made my remarks in 1967 until December of 1970, I had played with the idea of rewriting the Pledge in the form of a prayer.

A prayer looking forward to the day when America would be true to its dreams and to its hopes. A prayer that would look forward to America as a land of freedom and a land of justice and a land of liberty. The problem with that was, I don't like prayers in school. I knew that if the Pledge became a prayer, they would take it to schools and that I would have started something that I didn't like at all. But along came Look Magazine, certainly not an example of unfettered liberalism, with a Pledge of Allegiance written by Dr. James E. Allen, Jr., who happened to have been a former Commissioner of Education under President Dwight Eisenhower. He wrote the pledge this way:

> I pledge allegiance to the flag of the United States of America, and I dedicate myself to the principal that the republic for which it stands, shall be in truth, one nation, under God, indivisible, dedicated to liberty and justice for all.

If the pledge were written the way Dr. Allen suggested, then I should be pleased and proud to recite it. Why? Because what that wording does is put the responsibility for achieving America's goals, dreams, and ideals where that responsibility belongs: in the life of every American citizen. I dedicate myself to these principals, this pledge wording says.

I don't recite the pledge. Does that mean that I am not patriotic? Not by a long shot! I don't recite the pledge. Does that mean that I don't love my country? Not at all! By not reciting the pledge, in its present form, I may be demonstrating to the public at large that I love my country more than those who simply mouth those works unthinkingly. Listen again, to what Dr. Allen suggested. Listen and tell me whether this makes sense to you as an American citizen:

> I pledge allegiance to the flag of the United States of America, and I dedicate myself to the principal that the republic for which it stands, shall be in truth, one nation, under God, indivisible, dedicated to liberty and justice for all.

We aren't yet! Our American dream is 200 plus years old. I guess you might describe us as teenagers, and teenagers don't always have it all together. Well, we don't either. Our nation isn't yet what it could be, what it should be, what it dreams to be, what it sometimes, mistakenly, tells itself it already is. An act of repentance for me is to bring about change. An act of justice for me is to think about what's wrong with my nation and what needs to be corrected. We are a nation divided, racially, ethnically, religiously, economically, and in other ways. That's not what we want for America. That's not what America deserves. That's not what the flag represents.

So, at this time of the year, the time of the High Holidays, when we ask ourselves for acts of repentance, for prayer, and for acts of justice, I urge you to think of the one that I already perform. It will make you feel lonely at times, but it will also make you feel really good.

It just so happens that about twenty people from a neighboring community and their pastor visited our sanctuary that evening. They wanted to experience a little bit of Judaism about which they had been studying, particularly at the time of the High Holidays. Many of my congregants were upset and angry that I had delivered that sermon with non-Jews as our guests. The following Wednesday night was a Board meeting, and at the very beginning of the meeting some of the members of the Board began to take me to task for delivering that sermon on that particular night. At the first opportunity, I asked for permission to speak and read them a letter from the pastor of that church that was signed by almost everyone who had been in attendance. They had talked about my sermon in their bus going back to the community in which they lived. They found it to be very stimulating, very thought provoking, and quite spiritual and religious in its content. It was a totally new idea to them, and they greatly appreciated having been present in the sanctuary when it was discussed in my sermon. Those members of the Board of Trustees who had been angered quickly apologized and admitted their error. A couple of them even agreed that it had been a terrific sermon and that they had been wrong in believing that it had been inappropriate under the circumstances.

A sermon, entitled, "Our Biggest Enemy is Pride" was delivered at Beth Israel Congregation in Florence, South Carolina, on Friday, February 2, 1990. The first paragraph of that sermon reads as follows:

> I'm not sure how many years ago it was, but I know that it wasn't yesterday, that I saw a "Peanuts" cartoon strip. There were four panels or frames. In the first one, on a little hill, Charlie Brown and Lucy were standing and all that you could see was the back of them, looking past them out at the starry night, just black with little white dots representing the stars. In the next frame, it was as if the camera had pulled back a little, Charlie Brown and Lucy were smaller and there was a lot more sky. In the third frame was just sky. In the fourth frame you come back to a little teeny tiny Charlie Brown and Lucy, and Charlie Brown said, "Makes you feel kind of insignificant, doesn't it?" I remember that in whatever congregation I was

serving at the time I cut the cartoon out and put it up on the Bulletin Board in the synagogue, and I know that it stayed there for a while. I don't know where it is now. I hope that it is in one of my file folders somewhere. "Makes you feel kind of insignificant, doesn't it?" I think it would be terrific if we could really feel that way, because I suspect that is what gets in the way of our human spirituality, what gets in the way of our ability to approach God, what gets in the way of our ability to pray, is pride. I think pride is our greatest enemy.

In the middle of that sermon I described the *Shabbat* Walk which I do with kids at camp. That description is already in this book in a previous chapter. Then, the sermon continued:

I think that what really happens to those kids, if I do it right, is that we end up stripping away all the pretense and that they just simply are out there as human teenagers. Whether they are poor kids from the west side of Chicago or wealthy kids from Glencoe and other North Shore suburbs, whether they are wearing someone's hand me down jeans or a pair of designer jeans, $150 sneakers or $29.95 from K-Mart at that moment in time it just simply doesn't make a darn bit of difference. They are just human teenagers stripped of all pretenses. I am convinced that for that tiny bit of their lives, that half hour or 45 minutes, they begin to understand that they live their lives in relationship to another Power that exists in this universe. Pride is gone, for a little moment in time. Maybe, who knows, three years, five years later, twenty years later, one of those kids sitting in a synagogue somewhere, will hear the Rabbi say, "Let's open our *siddur* to page 617 and we will rise for the *Aleinu*", and those words will be recited. The kid will say, "Oh my God, I remember that. That crazy old man Rabbi that took us for a walk at night." Maybe the experience can be relived.

I don't know how to do that with you. You won't let me play those kinds of games with your head, and I have tried a couple of times. Maybe you need to do it for yourself. Somehow you need to discover that you are just simple, primal, human beings. Humanness. Understand that in this universe of which we are but a very tiny part, we do stand in relationship to another Power. Let's rid ourselves of everything that is an obstacle, that stands between us and that Power. I think that pride is the biggest.

Now, I want to quote two sermons for you in their entirety. The first one I witnessed and the second one was told to me by someone else. Early in my career in Peoria, probably during the spring of 1968, I delivered what I remembered to be a very forceful social action sermon. The president of the congregation was not present, but he must have received many phone calls during the week. Late on the following Friday afternoon, he called me and asked permission to say a word or two later that evening before my sermon. After the *Torah* had been returned to the Ark, I approached the lectern and introduced our president, Jack Szold. He walked forward, stood at the bottom of the steps to the *bimah*, and said the following:

> Some of you were concerned about the sermon the Rabbi delivered last week. If your religion doesn't make you itch in a place that you can't scratch, it isn't worth a damn.

With that, Jack sat down. I got up from my chair and turned toward our choir and said to Betty Ann Clayton, our music director, "Just sing the anthem." There was no way that I could preach after Jack's sermon.

In my second year in the rabbinate I met an old, gray haired, black preacher from a rural and very poor church. In one of our conversations he said to me,

> If your religion ain't no good on Monday, then it ain't no good on Sunday.

Doing Justice: Social Action

Within the first week of my arrival at Temple Beth El in Battle Creek, Michigan, I made my first courtesy call on a local mayor. We spent a few minutes just talking and beginning to get to know each other before he asked me if I would be willing to serve as a member of the Battle Creek Human Relations Commission. He told me that the ordinance establishing the commission had recently been passed by the City Commission and that he was still in the process of finding members. I told him that I was honored by his request and that I would be pleased to serve. I was somewhat frightened, but at the same time the invitation was a tremendous ego boost. Remember, I had been ordained only a month earlier and had been with my very first congregation for less than a week.

There were nine people who were appointed to this Commission. Three of us were clergy, one was the Director of the

101

United Way, another was the Executive of the Visiting Nurses Association, and the rest were people employed by businesses and industries in the community. I was elected vice chairman at the first meeting and eventually became chairman. I remained in Battle Creek for two and a half years and in retrospect feel that our Commission had a significant impact in three very different ways.

Firstly, some of us had pretty good connections with the local newspaper. Because of this, we were able to generate some important news stories along with regular reporting on our monthly meetings. This permitted us to get the messages of acceptance, positive intergroup relationships, and the idea that individual citizens needed to be involved in solving some of our local problems into the homes of our residents with a high degree of frequency. I am not sure that these newspaper articles had any significant or long lasting impact, but I do know that they generated immediate interest and response. My telephone rang frequently after a story about us appeared and there were always letters to the editor that were both positive and negative.

This led to our second significant accomplishment. We began to hear from some of the other communities in the state which had similar kinds of Commissions and as Commission members began to reach out to each other to discuss common problems. In early December 1961, our Commission hosted the first daylong workshop for Human Relations Commissioners for the state of Michigan. We had somewhere between 50 and 60 people in attendance on a Saturday. That annual session for Human

Relations Commissions continued at least throughout the 1960s, and then I lost touch with it.

This first annual program was held at the First United Methodist Church in downtown Battle Creek. As the vice chairman of our Commission, I held the primary responsibility for the programming of this workshop. It was scheduled to begin at 10:00 in the morning, and I was at the church before 9:30 just to make certain that everything was arranged the way I felt it should be. The physical structure of the building permitted direct access to the Fellowship Hall from street level. The sanctuary was one floor up, reached by a very imposing outdoor stairway. As I helped the custodian put finishing touches on the room arrangement and the continental breakfast, I asked him where I could find the ashtrays to distribute around the room. I was quite embarrassed when he replied that there was no smoking in a Methodist Church and that smoking was contrary to their belief system. That may have been my first practical knowledge learned in the field of intergroup relations. Then, with a beautiful smile on his face, he asked me to follow him upstairs. We ended up in the foyer in the main sanctuary, and he opened the doors at the top of that "imposing stairway." He took me to the low wall at the side edge of those steps and pointed down. There must have been a hundred cigarette butts on either side of those steps indicating that members of the First United Methodist Church flipped their cigarettes over the edge as they came into the building on Sunday mornings.

A third major accomplishment was in the area of housing. The woman who was the Director of the Visiting Nurses Association told us at a couple of our meetings that many of her nurses were disturbed by the very poor living conditions which they found in the homes and apartments occupied by their clients. She felt that this was a very significant problem that should be addressed by our Commission. Frankly, we didn't know what to do about it and it took us a long time to work our way around to the beginnings of a solution. In retrospect I must admit that I am quite pleased that all of us, who were so new to all of this, had enough stick-to-itiveness to keep working until we found a way in which we might be somewhat helpful. That attitude of continuing to discuss and peck away at a problem taught me a very valuable lesson about patience and frustration. Nonetheless, we eventually devised a brief one-page form that visiting nurses could carry on their clipboards. It permitted them to unobtrusively check off the condition of things such as plumbing, lighting, windows, screens, walls, ceilings, and floors each time they made a visit to a client. Each one of the forms likewise listed the address and/or apartment number.

At this time I became the chairman of the Commission. After we had approximately 100 individual visitations recorded, the director and I) took them to the official in city government who was responsible for building code enforcement. Our objective was to discover whether the city of Battle Creek was able to do anything relative to this substandard housing, most of it occupied by very low-income blacks. About fifteen minutes after our appointment began, he picked up his phone and asked the city attorney to come into his office. Now there were four of us involved. To shorten the story substantially, they selected fifty residents to focus upon. Building inspectors visited all fifty and letters from the code enforcement officials were then sent to all the property owners. Sixty days later they were inspected again and since none of the properties had been upgraded, letters were sent to the owners, this time by the city attorney. This time, the deadline was ninety days and a follow-up letter was sent giving a thirty day extension. At the end of that time period, approximately six months had passed. Much to our pleasure and amazement, significant improvement had been made by all the property owners except one. Two brothers owned six of the fifty dwellings. They had done nothing in the six months.

Unfortunately, they were members of my congregation. I'll follow up on this in a minute.

However, this approach taken by our Human Relations Commission, with strong support from the city government, clearly produced an almost instant improvement and success. We were quite proud of our accomplishment.

Now, about those two brothers who were members of Temple Beth El in Battle Creek. When this work of the Human Relations Commission had been completed, I spoke about the very significant accomplishments that had been made in terms of substandard housing for some of our citizens from the pulpit of my own congregation. Though I did not tape that sermon and therefore have no actual record of it, I do know very clearly the terrible mistake that I made. After reviewing everything that the Human Relations Commission had done, including our success with property owners, I concluded the sermon by saying something to the effect that there were two property owners who had refused to make any improvements at all in the houses which they rented to low income families. While I did not identify them by name, I said that they were both members of our synagogue and that they had embarrassed me greatly by their lack of willingness to do the proper, decent, and just thing. Those comments never should have been made.

Both gentlemen asked permission to come to the next board meeting and received it from our president, Herman Ginsberg. After the meeting had been opened, he gave them the floor and they told the board how angry they were at the concluding remarks of my sermon. They told me that I never should have said what I did, even if I felt that way. I interrupted to say that they were correct, and I apologized to them. That did not satisfy them. They demanded that the board check my sermons before they were delivered so that I would not say anything controversial or potentially embarrassing to any congregant. At that point, the president stopped them. He said that our synagogue had a free pulpit and that as the Rabbi of the synagogue I had the right to deliver any sermon that I chose. He added that in no way would he permit the board to censor my remarks in advance. The brothers, who were very hefty financial supporters of the congregation, said that then they would consider taking their dollars away from the synagogue and join another one somewhere else. To his great credit, the president stood up, looked them straight in the eye, and said, "That is your choice. Our congregation will not be blackmailed." Believe it or not, as far as I am aware, that was the end of that issue.

Shortly before that sermon I conducted a program on Friday night that was, quite literally, a sociodrama that involved the entire congregation. If you remember in the last chapter, I indicated that I always published the titles and a brief review of my sermons in advance. That was also done for this *Erev Shabbat*. However, on Tuesday of that week we sent a postcard to all the members that was signed by the president. It said that something very special had come up and that the Rabbi had decided that we needed to have a full discussion on Friday night. Therefore, I would not be delivering my sermon. The discussion was to take place downstairs in the Social Hall before the *Oneg Shabbat*. I reminded people of that when they came to services on Friday night and unbeknownst to them, with the collusion of the president and three congregants, we were about to conduct a program which had been published by the Commission on Social Action of Reform Judaism entitled, *The Three Sons*.

When our congregants got downstairs after services, they found chairs set up in auditorium style facing the stage. The president got up on the stage and showed them a letter we had faked that used the letterhead of the URJ. The letter said that a very prominent Jew who had three adult sons had died and left a substantial estate that was to be given to whichever son the Jewish community considered to be the best Jew. Supposedly, our congregation was one of a number that had been chosen to listen to descriptions of all three sons' lives. . We had been asked to take a vote and send the results to the national offices of the Union for Reform Judaism. With that, the president opened the curtains on the stage and revealed a banquet table with three chairs behind it. In front of each chair was a placard with the first name of each son. Three members of the congregation were introduced, and they took their places at the table. The president said that each had a biographical statement of one of the sons, and that each would describe the son to us for no longer than three minutes. When all three were finished, we would permit four or five minutes of direct questions from the audience to these three congregants. When that was completed, we would open the floor for general discussion prior to taking the vote. We used a script that had been prepared by the Commission on Social Action. Each one of the sons had some very positive attributes from Judaism's point of view, yet each had also demonstrated behavior that could have been considered unjust or contrary to what the Commission on Social Action condoned. There was no black and white, just a great deal of gray. This meant that the congregants had to establish priorities for themselves to determine what behavior was more acceptable.

The program worked very well and a very spirited discussion followed. Ballots were distributed, everybody voted, and then refreshments were served for the *Oneg Shabbat*. I went into my office and tabulated the ballots with assistance from the president. We then came out onto the stage and the president announced the decision. The vote was very close. As I recall, approximately sixty people were present and the winner did not receive a majority of the votes cast. Then I told the congregants that the whole thing was a put-up job and that it was a program developed by our Commission on Social Action. I explained that we ran it as we did in an attempt to increase their level of involvement by making it seem more real to them. Some of the congregants were quite upset. Others thought it was a terrific way to create and stimulate significant discussion.

My brother-in-law eventually married a young woman from Battle Creek, and his mother-in-law had been present in our sanctuary and Social Hall when *The Three Sons* was presented. I have seen Betty many times since I left Battle Creek, because by extension she was a member of the family. Virtually every time I saw her she said something like, "you SOB, you sure did make all of us feel foolish the night you made us take a vote."

It was always easy to get congregations and congregants, individually or in small groups, to talk about the issues of social action; yet it was very difficult to get my congregations and congregants involved in any significant way. Everyone tends to agree that Judaism is much more than ritual, worship, and observances. However, we seem to frequently fall into the "Let George do it" syndrome. Or as I have otherwise called it, the "vicarious Jew" syndrome, with the Rabbi most often being the vicarious one. There seems to be a three-step thought process going on:

1. I know Judaism expects righteousness and justice.

2. The Rabbi and some others seem to be taking care of it.

3. Therefore, I don't have to be involved and I can still feel comfortable.

These beliefs are coupled with the attitude that says it is perfectly OK for individual Jews to be involved in efforts toward *Tikkun Olam* (the repair of the world), but it is not proper for corporate Judaism or the synagogue to involve itself in a similar way. According to this view, it mixes religion and politics and we ought to stay out of it. Frankly, I was always impressed with how my politically conservative congregants were so concerned about the place of religion in national life when that religion was Judaism or when they considered the possibility of involvement in some sort of social action issue. However, they never seemed to be concerned about Christians' incursions into the political arena and how they used the political process to reach their own agenda or goals. Jewish conservatives today still complain about our Social Action Commission, but never about the Christian Coalition. Most of the religious community is immune from criticism by these folks, not their own!

A variance of that idea which I heard expressed very, very often in the early days of my career was that our involvement in the community would foster additional anti-Semitism. I never believed it and addressed my concern with this issue to various people on the staff of the Commission of Social Action of the URJ. They could provide me with no significant documentation that anti-Semitism followed the involvement of Jews or Judaism in social action. Neither could various regional representatives of the Anti-Defamation League. That truth never seemed to deter those who used anti-Semitism as their rationalization for noninvolvement in social action issues. During the days of the civil rights struggle, I would have been so happy to have simply heard a congregant say, "Rabbi, I don't want you or the congregation involved in any of this stuff. It's got nothing to do with Judaism. I just don't like colored people." That kind of honesty would have been refreshing.

On a personal level, I was involved in some significant civil rights activities and protests. Kenosha, Wisconsin was a blue-collar town with a very poor record of its treatment of black citizens. Housing was segregated while employment and advancement opportunities were difficult at best. Black people who became my friends, visited my home, and had me in theirs told me that I was one of the few white people with whom they ever spent any time unless it was under the auspices of some community or civic organization. To draw attention to these issues, some of my friends and I organized a march through downtown Kenosha that began at the synagogue and ended up at a public park. We heard all sorts of dire predictions about how we would be mistreated by people on the sidewalks and how we would be threatened with physical harm if we went ahead with our plans. Almost the exact opposite was true. About a hundred of us started to walk and when we got to the park there were almost 250 people. In other words, folks just stepped off the sidewalk and joined us in our march down the street. It was a wonderfully gratifying example of good people coming together for a good cause. The following morning the newspaper made a big deal of the fact that the number of participants had gone up by two and a half times in the mile and a half or so that it took for the march.

In the same town and at the same time, I took on another issue that was quite personal to me as the Rabbi of the Jewish community. I am convinced that this issue was much more dangerous. When I arrived in Kenosha in the spring of 1962, there was one dilapidated and dying hotel which closed very soon thereafter. There were no motels at which I would have been comfortable staying, and there were no public facilities for meetings and so forth except for the ballroom in the Elks Club building. Virtually every organization in town that had meetings held them at the Elks Club: the Rotary, Kiwanis, Bar Association, Hospital Auxiliary, Symphony League, Dental Association, county physicians' group, and everyone else you could think of. The problem was that in a community with outstanding Jewish civic leadership, no Jew had ever been a member of the Elks Club and it was very well understood that no Jew would ever be permitted to be a member. Because Jews, myself included, desired to be active in the community, we needed to swallow our pride and attend functions held at the Elks Club. There was no way to be involved and to have remained outside of that building.

Eventually and thankfully, a motel chain opened a building in town which had banquet facilities suitable for most of the organizations that met at the Elks. In fact, the Rotary Club to which I belonged met in this motel while the Elks Club ballroom was being refurbished. Now that there was an alternative, the

Jewish community was faced with making the discrimination at the Elks Club an issue or continue to permit themselves to be discriminated against without protest.

My next-door neighbor was a Polish Catholic by the name of Leonard "Len" Czerniec. He was a member of the Elks Club and invited me to join him there for lunch. When I refused the third time, he asked me what was going on and so I told him the story. He suggested, "Well, let's get some important Jewish guys and sponsor them for membership and see what happens." He told me that if I was right and these people were blackballed, he would support me in any public protest that I made. Since all these things came together at one time, it seemed opportune to do something. I found a group of Jews who were willing to submit their names for membership in the Elks Club. They included:

1. the most prominent Realtor in town
2. the owner of the only radio station in town
3. the publisher of the local newspaper
4. two very prominent attorneys who had, between them, chaired virtually every important civic organization in the community
5. the chairman of the local school board
6. two or three downtown merchants

Obviously, these were people who should have been sought after and embraced for membership in any organization.

My friend Len found sponsors for each of these people. The paperwork was completed, submitted, and everybody was blackballed. At that point, I went to the president of my Rotary Club and suggested that since four of the group that had been blackballed for membership in the Elks Club were members of Rotary, it would be appropriate if Rotary supported them by changing its meeting place to the motel which had already accommodated us for a month or so. He understood exactly what I was suggesting and offered his personal support. He asked me to attend the next meeting of the Board of the Rotary Club and present my suggestion formally. I did that and left the meeting. I was notified by the president within an hour that my request had been turned down.

Then I had some real work to do. I wanted to make this a public issue, and I needed the support of all the gentlemen who had been blackballed. I also needed the support of the local newspaper. I intended to resign from Rotary publicly (which met at noon on Friday) and deliver a sermon in my synagogue that same Friday night with full exposure and media coverage.

Everything went well. While all of this was in the planning stage, a Wisconsin Supreme Court Justice announced his refusal to attend meetings and social gatherings in one of the private clubs in Madison because he had learned it refused admittance to Jews and blacks. That gave me exactly the kind of public encouragement that I needed. It also created the media attention that I desired.

All the gentlemen who had subjected themselves to the public humiliation of being blackballed for membership in the Elks Club permitted me to use their names publicly. All applauded my decision to go public with my resignation from the Rotary Club and the reason for it. However, the publisher of the local newspaper told me that he would not permit his newspaper to cover the story. A few days later, one of his editors told me that the publisher was concerned about a drop in advertising revenue if the community felt that the newspaper was attacking the Elks Club. Since I had the permission of the gentlemen involved, I then announced a sermon in my congregational Bulletin, as was my usual practice, entitled, "Why I Resigned from Rotary Today." I called the editors of the newspapers in Madison and in Milwaukee and contacted the TV stations in both communities as well. They all agreed to cover my sermon. Two of the television stations arranged to do an interview with me on Friday afternoon to use on their local news at 6:00 p.m.

Slowly, the word spread through town and I received a few phone calls from Rotary members. Some asked if I would permit them to attend my services on Friday night because they felt that what I was doing was proper. Others condemned my actions and thought that I was doing a great injustice to our community.

On the Friday that I had chosen, I attended the Rotary meeting and sat at my usual table. Before the scheduled program, the president introduced me to make a few remarks. I walked to the head table and I announced my resignation from Rotary. I explained that I had joined the Rotary Club even though it met in

115

the Elks Club building because when I arrived in Kenosha in the spring of 1962 there was no other option. I reminded the Rotarians that we had met in another facility and that an option now existed. Since a large group of my congregants had been blackballed by the Elks Club membership, I felt that I could no longer attend meetings held in that building. Furthermore, I pointed out that four of those who had been blackballed were my fellow Rotarians. I walked out of the meeting and all the Jewish Rotarians who had been blackballed by the Elks Club walked out with me. Unbeknownst to me, they had submitted their resignations in writing the same day. I was surprised and overwhelmed by that support.

However, as we were walking out of the room, one of my other congregants stood up and said out loud, "I am very unhappy with the decision that the Rabbi made. I am certainly not going to resign from Rotary, and I am certainly going to continue to attend functions in this building." One of the men who was walking out with me said, "Harry, could that be because you are a liquor wholesaler and the Elks Club is one of your major accounts?" During the afternoon, bomb threats were phoned to the synagogue as well as to my home. After *Shabbat* dinner, my three children were taken to a neighbor's home for the evening and we went on to services.

I also invited a number of my friends in the Christian clergy to attend that night as a show of support. Approximately twenty ministers, priests, and nuns were there, most of them quite identifiable by their clerical dress. The sermon basically repeated the message that I had delivered to Rotary earlier in the day. It talked about the pride of Jewishness and the necessity, on occasion, of standing up to be counted as a Jew. At the same time, it mentioned the obligation to refuse to participate in acts of discrimination. I concluded by asking the members of my congregation (most of whom were in attendance as if it were *Kol Nidre* night) to consider their own behavior in terms of continued participation in the organizations to which they belonged. I asked the physicians how they could continue to go to meetings and other kinds of social functions at the Elks Club, when so many members of their congregation had been refused membership in the Elks Club. "How can we continue to support an organization with our dollars and with our presence when we know the organization refuses to accept us as members?"

My call for a boycott was featured heavily on the 10:00 news that Friday night in both Madison and Milwaukee. My verbal protest was front page news in both communities on Saturday.

I did not know that the writers and editorial staff of the newspaper in Kenosha had prepared full coverage of these events, along with photos and biographies focused on the level of civic involvement of the members of my congregation who had been blackballed. That article ran on Saturday morning as well, because the publisher happened to have been out of town on vacation. Incidentally, I was presented with the "Page One Award" by the members of the Kenosha Newspaper Guild on January 25, 1966. The citation read: "For many outstanding services to the community consistent with the highest ideals of the American newspaper guild." The plaque was presented to me at a dinner at the motel and attended by most of the men whose membership in the Elks Club had been denied, including the newspaper publisher who obviously had a change of heart. I guess his advertising revenue didn't drop.

I left Kenosha at the end of June 1966 to go to Peoria, Illinois. Therefore, I can only relate the conclusion to the story as secondhand information. Since my friend Len Czerniec was very much involved, I can vouch for its veracity. Following the blackballing of the Jewish men and my making the entire incident public, Len spoke to all of those who had served as the sponsors for my congregants. They agreed that at least three of them would attend every single Elks Club meeting and would continuously blackball everybody proposed for membership. This would be their way to indicate their displeasure with the blackballing of Jews, and with the use of a blackball for membership in general.

Shortly after I left the community, Len was told that the liquor license of the Elks Club was coming up for renewal by the city government. Obviously, such renewal is usually automatic. Len and some of the others involved in this process immediately went to see the mayor and indicated that they would be very displeased if that liquor license was renewed given the obvious discriminatory practices of the Elks Club. The mayor and some of the members of the city council sat down to talk with the Elks' Exalted Ruler, explaining to him the very difficult circumstances in which they as elected officials had been placed by the discriminatory membership policies of the Elks Club. The Exalted Ruler agreed to convene a meeting of the Elks Club leadership to resolve this problem. The meeting was held in city hall and the primary agenda was a full discussion of the ramifications caused by the behavior of the Elks Club. The leadership of the Elks Club stated that they agreed completely with the stand taken by the city government and simply asked for a three-month extension of their liquor license so that they could solve the problem internally. That compromise was accepted by the mayor with the understanding that he would bring it to the attention of the media so that the entire community would know that city government did not concur with the discriminatory policies of the Elks Club.

There are two conclusions to this story. One is that the leadership of the Kenosha Elks Club managed to solve the problem of Jews being blackballed and three or four were immediately admitted membership. I have been told that a significant number of others became members later. Much more importantly and surprisingly, a few years later the Kenosha Elks Club led the fight in the state of Wisconsin to remove the "whites only" clause in the statewide membership policies of Elkdom. They were successful, and I believe this eventually became national policy.

While you have just read a long story, it took much longer to work its way out. There were times when it was filled with a great deal of tension. There were times when it involved a tremendous amount of hard work. There were times when those of us involved were very frightened. But, in the end the desired result was achieved and we all ended up feeling quite good.

On January 17, 1964, while I was serving Beth Hillel in Kenosha, I delivered a sermon entitled, "Have We Not All One Father?" Please realize the date of the sermon and remember that quotations from the liturgy are in the stylized English of *The Union Prayer Book, Newly Revised, Volume I*. This sermon attempted to explain social action to that congregation, and it began this way:

> "*Sh'ma Yisrael*. Two times tonight we have recited and sung those words, "Hear, Oh Israel, The Lord our God, the Lord is One." Two times, each time we come into this sanctuary. This is proclaimed as the watchword of our faith. This is the core of our beliefs. And then, as we went through our service we said, "Have we not all one father? Hath not one God created us?" Then, "Why do we deal treacherously brother against brother?" How easy it is, how very easy for us to mouth the words, for us to say, "The Lord our God, the Lord is One," without pausing to consider any of the ramifications of our concept of a unitary, creating God. If God is one, then our universe is likewise one, humanity is one and we are brothers. That should be sufficient rationale for a congregation such as ours, for any congregation adhering to the Jewish faith, to involve itself in the work of social

action. "The Lord is One." "Have we not all one Father?" The statement and the question should be enough. Unfortunately, they most probably are not and so we spend this evening looking at this topic of social action finding out what it is, and why it belongs here in this congregation.

In an effort to find an adequate definition of social action, I turned to some material prepared by the Commission on Social Action and used their definition:

> Social Action is the contemporary counterpart of the dedication to social justice which characterized the prophets of Israel. They condemned injustice wherever it appeared, whether in the marketplace or political arena, for they were impelled by the moral imperative of Judaism. Social action is the process through which the ethical principles of Judaism are put to work in the solution of social problems in our communities, the nation, and the world. This is not politics or sociology or economics. It involves the essence of religion, the Jewish religion. It requires of us, not only stirring sermons of the Rabbi, but effective grassroots action by the men and women who make up the congregation. This is social action.

I then continued with an analysis of a quotation from the great Rabbi, Hillel.

Let's begin with the man for whom this congregation is named. Let's begin with that great Rabbi of the first pre-Christian century, Hillel. The quotation is one with which you are most certainly already familiar. "If I am not for myself who will be for me." That's right. We can't deny that. Every one of us must be interested in our own destiny, in our own future, our own progress, our own success, our own health, of necessity, we concern ourselves with ourselves. And we admit it, for if we don't care, who will, as Hillel says. But then he goes on, "Yet if I am for myself only, what am I?" What am I? Can we be completely self-centered and be human? Can we be completely self-centered and be truly a Jew? Hillel certainly would have answered those questions in the negative. He obviously must have felt that every man's area of concern extends way beyond himself. Every man would be his brother's keeper. And then, Hillel attacks what we so often fall prey to, and he says, "If not now, when?" "Oh yes, I agree with you Rabbi, of course you're right, but you see, I'm just a little too busy now." "I can't do it this week, maybe I'll find time next week." "I'd like to help out but, no, we're doing some work at the store. I think I better say no this time, but I agree with you." Hillel said, twenty-one centuries ago what the American Negro is saying now. The time is now. The time is always now! Tomorrow is always too late. When the call rings out, when the challenge comes, we must answer with Hillel. We must say, if not now, if I can't do it now, if I'm too busy now, if I'm too involved now, if I can't care enough now, when will I care?

I then continued with a short review of some additional rabbinic literature, quoted from the Pittsburgh Platform of the CCAR from 1885 and moved on to the Guiding Principles of American Reform Judaism as drawn up by the CCAR in 1937. I quoted one sentence, "Judaism seeks the attainment of a just society by the application of its teachings to the economic order, to industry and commerce, to national and international affairs." I then went on with these words:

> But note, this is active, this is not a passive statement. This isn't a prayer addressed to God, "O God, I wish there was a better world in which to live." It isn't that at all. Judaism seeks, it says, seeks to obtain a better society by applying its own teachings. And you cannot seek, and you cannot apply by being passive. In Columbus, Ohio, in 1937, when they wrote the Guiding Principles, they were talking about social action for American Reform Judaism. They were talking about American Reform Jews seeking and applying themselves and the principles of their faith to the problems of their society, seeking solutions in terms of the just, in terms of the merciful, in terms of the righteous.

After some additional comments that followed the same thought, I continued in this way:

> Rabbi Roland Gittelsohn, one of the foremost American Reform Rabbis, preaching a sermon to his congregation (Temple Israel, Boston) on this topic said these things:
>
>> Isn't there a certain amount of risk attached to this area of congregational activity? Aren't some of the subjects with which the Social Action Committee would concern itself controversial? The only answer to these questions is in the affirmative. Yes. There is an element of risk. Yes. Some of the subjects are apt to be controversial.
>
> These questions were answered by Dr. Maurice N. Eisendrath, president of the Union for Reform Judaism, when he said:
>
>> What kind of Judaism can conceivably be worthy of its proud name and heritage if it does not encounter difficulties in a time of moral and spiritual deterioration such

as our own? Any religious organization or religious enterprise that stays out of trouble in such a day, cannot be but false to its pristine purposes and prophetic past.

Rabbi Gittelsohn admits that there is risk and will be controversy and Dr. Eisendrath says there must be risk and controversy in any faith that is vital, for life itself entails risk. Life itself entails difficulty and conflicts. We can either get in there with our religion or we can divorce our religion completely.

Doesn't that sound very much like the sermon that Jack Szold delivered in our congregation in Peoria? If you don't remember, look back at the end of the previous chapter.

My sermon ended with these words:

This is social action. This is the essence of our religion. Involvement in the day-to-day concerns of our society by working through the synagogue, through the temples such as Beth Hillel for the advancement of social justice. We bridge the gap between confession and commitment, between word and deed and in the end, we fulfill ourselves as Jews. This is social action in the synagogue. It is the most modern and effective expression I know of a message preached so eloquently by the ancient Hebrew prophets, *Va-yig-ba Adonai tz'va-ot ba-mish-pat, v'ha-eil ha-ka-dosh nik-dash bitz-da-kah.* The Lord of Hosts is exalted through justice and God, the Holy One, is sanctified through our righteousness.

No matter how "brilliant" my social action sermon might have been, I learned two other exceedingly important lessons while I was still the Rabbi in Kenosha. Firstly, I helped start a human relations membership organization with my friend Tom Anger who was a professional photographer and Roman Catholic. The community had a Human Relations Commission, of which I was a member. However, it did not have significant support from elected government officials, and it was basically a nonproductive figurehead. Tom and I both felt that it would be vitally important to get as many citizens involved in human relations activities and discussions as we possibly could if we ever hoped to have any sort of impact on the community. It was very slow going at first, but eventually we had a core group of black and white citizens that numbered approximately thirty. By the time I left Kenosha in the summer of 1966, the membership was up to over 100. Our first few meetings simply were brainstorm discussions, with everybody describing problems and a few tentative suggestions for solutions. At the third meeting, one woman spoke up and said that she kept hearing one refrain over and over during the first two sessions. She reminded us that people had constantly said that they didn't really know anybody from the other racial group. They might work together, but they didn't know each other. I specifically remember her comment directed at one of the other women in the group, "Marilyn and I have worked together for almost five years in the same office. We talk to each other each day, but I don't know anything about her and I'm rather certain that she doesn't know anything about me. How can things get better when even people who work together don't know each other?" That remark set us off. We created small husband and wife interracial discussion groups that met a minimum of once per month, first in the home of one family and then in the home of another, always alternating the race of the host. There was no specific agenda. We simply had to talk about our lives, our dreams, and our fears.

Clearly, it took a while for people to develop significantly trusting relationships with others that they did not really know. However, reports indicated that by the third or fourth session, people began to speak from the heart and share their true feelings and experiences. I remember sitting in a black family's home and one of the gentlemen who was a middle manager in a local factory told us about the fear and the very real unpleasant experiences involved in taking his family on an automobile vacation through Wisconsin and Minnesota. Even though the civil rights movement was by now very well established, and even though most of us who were white assumed that the problems were basically in the South, he related how difficult it was to plan a trip. He had to be sure that he and his family would be welcome at motels, restaurants, and places where they wanted to stop for sightseeing. He described how he talked with other blacks whom he knew to discover where they had stayed, eaten, and felt comfortable. He probably talked for five or six minutes. Throughout his comments, I kept saying to myself that can't be happening in these two northern states and I certainly don't have any of those concerns when I pile my family in the car for any kind of trip. When he finished, many of the other blacks in the group expressed exactly the same fears. It was an eye opener that was frightening in its reality.

As I think back, I am reminded of a story that Harry Golden, publisher of the *Carolina Israelite*, once told in his book, *Only In America*. He related the story of a school bus driver who stopped to pick up a black kindergarten child on her first day of school. When he opened the door to the bus, he heard the mother say to her daughter, "Remember, honey, you have to sit all the way in the back of the bus." If I remember correctly, Golden related that the bus driver quit immediately. As I listened to my newfound black friends, I understood that sentiment and felt the same kind of both embarrassment and shock.

The other lesson that I learned taught me of the total viciousness that people can express to others under certain circumstances. I had been invited by a black minister to come to the basement of his church to help train some of his older teenagers for what they might experience on a freedom ride into the South. Just as I described in an earlier chapter, he set up a fake restaurant counter and had five or six of his black teenagers role play a sit-in. We, the white adults, were told to vilify those kids, to scream at them, to swear at them, to spit on them. He wanted his students to know what they would experience in the deep South.

It took me a while to get into the swing of things, and while I felt very strange, I thought I was doing an effective job. He tapped me on the shoulder and beckoned for me to move away. He said to me, "Larry, forget your morality. Forget that you are a Rabbi. Drop your inhibitions and really let those kids have it." I thought that I had been exceedingly mean but he thought that I had not been forceful enough. I went back to my place, stood behind those black teenagers, and really began to act. I quite literally frightened myself and after only three or four minutes I had to stop. When I got my emotions back under control, I did it all over again and this time was able to keep it up for the ten or fifteen minutes until the session ended. All of us attempted to apologize to the kids, but that black clergyman wouldn't permit us to do so. He reminded those teenagers that they needed to know what to expect. He told them that what we had heaped on them would probably be mild compared to the reality that they were about to experience. I can't remember ever feeling so despondent. It was probably one of the lowest points in my entire existence because it made me humanize a complete lack of humanity.

I remember another story that was quite current during the early 1960s. Because I am not certain of all the details, I will not name the community, congregation, or rabbi involved. One of my colleagues had seemingly involved himself in a freedom ride and sit-in held in the Deep South during the days of the Civil Rights protest. He was arrested along with many other clergy and called his wife with his one phone call. She, in turn, called the president of the congregation. In his wisdom, he called an emergency meeting of the congregational board for that evening.

Allegedly, the board promptly fired the rabbi. However, in the morning when the newspaper came out with the report of the arrest of this group of clergy, the headlines indicated that one of the Rockefellers, who was an Episcopal Priest, was also arrested. He seemed to have enough *Yichus*, and his participation and arrest legitimized the involvement of my rabbinic friend. The Board met again, and promptly rehired him.

On many occasions I served as a member of an NAACP Board, and twice on the State Board. I represented the Chicago office of the URJ on Project Equality of Illinois. On three different occasions I was a member of the State Board of the ACLU, and on two separate occasions, a member of the ADL Regional Advisory Board. I chaired the Social Action and the Church-State committees for the St. Louis Rabbinical Association. I was a board member of the St. Louis Jewish Community Relations Council and a member of their Church-State Committee.

Therefore, I can feel rather proud of my involvement in social action issues, but I am quite disappointed in my lack of ability to motivate members of my congregation to be involved. Even before the URJ developed its program of collecting canned, boxed, and bottled foods for distribution to the needy on *Yom Kippur*, I had started such a program in my congregation. We ran it from *Erev Rosh HaShanah* through the end of *Sukkot*, with the primary slogan, "We Fast So That Others Might Eat." Over the course of the years we averaged about five pounds of food donated for each adult congregant. However, it wasn't until after the High Holidays in 1996 that I was able to convince some congregants to take the food directly to the Food Bank and have some minimal level of interaction with those who benefited from the Food Bank's help.

On one occasion in Florence, we brought an infant's crib into the Social Hall and ran a campaign to load it up with items for infants. We filled it and the floor around it quickly, but I had a difficult time convincing anybody to come with me to the shelter for battered women and children to deliver it.

It appears to be easy to collect money, food, and baby items and bring them to the synagogue, but very difficult to get the congregation outside of its own building. Other rabbis are quite successful, and many congregations have developed extraordinarily useful social action programming. There must have been some failings in my personality that made it impossible for me to duplicate those activities in the congregations which I served. Or maybe it was a factor of my serving small congregations, without sufficient numbers to carry out an active, ongoing program. However, in Dothan, Alabama, our small congregation joined with Evergreen Presbyterian Church to build two homes for Habitat for Humanity. The pastor of that church is my very good friend, Joe Johnson. I'm glad that I can end this chapter on a happy, upbeat note.

The JCS Made Me A Star

As I reread the things that I have already written, I realize that I do brag more than a little. This is because I have been very pleased with my career in the rabbinate. However, one aspect of my career has given me considerably more pleasure than any other. That is the teaching that I did, whether it was within the congregation, a parochial high school, or a variety of colleges and universities.

In the summer of 1966 when I moved to Peoria, I was asked by our sister congregation in Bloomington, Illinois whether I would be willing to accept two extra assignments. One was a chaplaincy at the Lincoln State School and the other was teaching at Illinois Wesleyan University in Normal, Illinois. Lincoln State School was a facility for the mentally handicapped, which I served once each week. Both activities were usually covered by the Reform rabbi in Bloomington, but the congregation was without full time rabbinic service for two years and I filled in.

I taught one course in the spring semester in 1967 and again in 1968. My course was, "An Introduction to Judaism" and I used Bernard Bamberger's *The Story of Judaism*. I had only finished my education less than eight years before I first began to teach and I was quite frightened. In the months preceding my first class, I thought back to my days at HUC trying to discover what had impressed me about the various faculty members who were my professors and what had disturbed or distressed me. I went so far as to make a list of the positives and the negatives, and I tried my very best to emulate the positives. I must have been relatively successful, because the feedback from student evaluations was quite positive.

I discovered one very interesting problem at the end of my first semester of teaching. A couple of days before the last class, the students began to ask me what the final exam was going to be about. Of course, my first offhand response was that it would cover everything we had dealt with during the course. I quickly realized that the response was inadequate and inaccurate, yet I didn't feel that I could be very specific because that would give away the content of the exam. I did tell the students that it would involve definitions of the many important terms which I had introduced to them and that all the other questions would be in essay form. I then suggested that they spend most of their study time on the topics that appeared to them to be of major importance. The final exam results were somewhat uneven. It quickly occurred to me that in their efforts to determine which topics were most important, some students had guessed wrong. They all knew the material, but some of them had not prepared themselves to answer the specific questions that I asked. So, for the second year that I taught, I gave the students a copy of the final exam on the last day of class. I told them that I understood that they couldn't restudy everything which we had discussed and I indicated that I was in a better position to determine what was important than they were. Therefore, I simply gave them the exam questions in advance. I assumed that if they would seriously prepare themselves to answer those questions, they would have the knowledge at the end of the course that I felt was important for them to have. I used that technique in every course that I taught, with what I think was very good success.

On the very first day of the very first class that I taught at Illinois Weslyan, one of the students who arrived early talked to me about the course and presented me with one of his pet peeves. He said that he really disliked professors who lectured from the textbook. He felt that those teachers didn't respect the students because they assumed that the students were incapable of reading the book on their own and learning what it contained. That was an interesting idea which I had never previously considered. When the class met for the second time and after I had distributed a course calendar and reading assignment list, I suggested that at the opening of each class I would permit the students to ask me questions based on the readings that had been assigned for that date. When that portion of our time together was over, I moved on to my own teaching agenda. That worked very well, and I continued to use that specific method in all my teaching whether on the college or congregational level.

My teaching at Illinois Wesleyan University was sponsored by the Jewish Chautauqua Society (JCS), which is an important arm of the National Federation of Temple Brotherhoods. Its main idea is that anti-Semitism and misunderstandings about Judaism can be offset, diminished, and hopefully eliminated by teaching the next generation's opinion makers about Judaism in a formal college class setting. I taught for the JCS in several different locations, and I truly believe that their concept works. I firmly believe that the organization has made an outstanding contribution to intergroup relations in the United States and that its impact will continue to be felt down through the generations. Dollar for dollar, it may well be the best investment ever made by the American Jewish community.

While the "resident lectureship" (the full college course taught by a Rabbi) may be the program with the highest impact run by the JCS, many other programs are quite valuable as well. JCS made rabbis available for short visits to college campuses and I fulfilled a lot of those assignments. Sometimes it meant one day on campus and sometimes it stretched out to three or four. The object was to spend as much time in class with the students as possible lecturing and/or answering their questions about Jews and Judaism. Frequently the classes were in the departments of religious studies, history, sociology/psychology, literature, or even Holocaust studies. The rabbi was considered to be the "expert." They cleared up misunderstandings and presented factual information which frequently was beyond the knowledge base of the professor teaching the class. Just as importantly, this may have been the one and only time in their lives when some of these students from small towns in mid-America ever had the opportunity of interacting directly with a rabbi. In some cases, this was the first opportunity for these students to actually meet and speak with any Jew.

In the summer of 1984, when I moved to Beth Israel Congregation in Florence, South Carolina, I was contacted by the chairman of the Religious Studies Department of St. Andrews Presbyterian College in Laurinburg, North Carolina. It was a small college with approximately 650 students. This individual had recently come to St. Andrews from a college in Tennessee that had been served by a JCS Resident Lecturer. He had applied for and awarded a grant from JCS to employ a Rabbi to teach a for-credit course during the spring semester. He asked me if I was interested in being the faculty person for that course. I assured him that I was, and I told him that I had already done that at Illinois Wesleyan University in Normal for two years in the 1960s. We arranged for me to drive up to St. Andrews (which was approximately 65 miles north of Florence) to meet and discuss what I would be comfortable doing for them. At that meeting, I was introduced to other faculty members as well as to the President and Vice President for Academic Affairs. We decided that in the spring semester of 1985 I would teach a two-credit course entitled, *An Introduction to Judaism*. The textbooks that I selected were Steinberg's *Basic Judaism* and Bamberger's *The Story of Judaism*. The decision to employ me as a part time faculty member came too late for my courses to be included in the listing of courses for the 1984-85 school year. Therefore, prior to registration in December for the spring semester, the department chairman plastered the school with posters and arranged for me to be interviewed by the student newspaper. That article appeared just before registration. To everyone's surprise, that publicity effort resulted in a registration of over thirty students. I offered one course each spring semester through the spring of 1994, which totaled to ten years. Eventually, I rotated three courses: *An Introduction to Judaism, An Overview of the Hebrew Bible* using Samuel Sandmel's *The Hebrew Scriptures*, and *The Jewish Experience in America* using the four-volume set *Eyewitnesses to American Jewish History* written by Eisenberg and Goodman and published by the URJ.

In all three courses, one of the requirements was for students to visit the synagogue in Florence for a service on *Erev Shabbat*. I encouraged my students to attend services on the third Friday night in February which was a special presentation entitled, "Neighbor Night." More will be written about that later. It is enough to say at this time that it was a service to which my congregants were urged to invite their non-Jewish neighbors, friends, and business associates. The service was explained as it was conducted. There was no sermon, but for approximately twenty minutes after the liturgy was concluded, our guests were invited to ask me questions. That seemed to be the most appropriate time for my students to join us in worship.

After I had taught at St. Andrews for four years, the Religious Studies Department determined that anyone who majored in religion had to take at least one of the courses that I offered. That was later changed to a requirement for two of the three courses. My classes were always very well attended, and I believe that my experience was very valuable to the students as well as to the faculty.

On several occasions, I was invited to attend faculty meetings to present to the professors on a subject chosen either by me or based on previous discussions held by the faculty. I considered this to be quite unusual and quite an honor. The staff of the JCS agreed that it was very unusual and very extraordinary for the college to require my course for students who were studying for a major in religion.

The only students that ever presented me with any kind of significant difficulty in my classes at St. Andrews were those who were Jewish. Somehow or other they felt that there was no need to study, very little need to participate, and very little need to attend classes. I assumed that they felt their childhood religious education programs would get them through the course with a good grade. Unfortunately, they were frequently mistaken.

In the spring of 1990, the New York staff of the JCS decided to produce a promotional video that would be used by NFTB chapters in Reform congregations throughout the United States and Canada. Three resident lecturers were selected to appear in that video, and I was fortunate enough to be one of them. The video was released in the fall of 1991 and was entitled, "Honest Differences, Common Ground."

We began our shoot on a Thursday at my home in Florence with me simply talking about the value that I found in teaching on the campus at St. Andrews Presbyterian College. Then we drove up to the campus.

I had arranged for the use of a classroom and had invited as many of my current students to sit in on a mock class as could make it. I promised them that they would be featured in a video which would have national exposure. Approximately twenty students showed up. While the cameras were running I lectured, drew on the board in colored chalk, asked questions, and ran a class discussion. My students were very cooperative and I felt comfortable when that part of our work was completed.

On Friday, the entire camera crew came to my office and did another interview that primarily asked me to discuss what I considered to be the impact of the JCS's work on college campuses. I not only had served as a resident lecturer, but I had fulfilled many of the one, two, and three-day visitations throughout the Midwest and the south. Lastly, I asked my current and previous students to attend services that Friday evening and the crew videotaped some additional footage with the permission of the Board of Trustees. All in all we ended up with approximately four hours of material on tape. The final video runs a little less than fifteen minutes and material from that four hours occupies about one-third of the finished product. The video was released in the fall of 1991 to coincide with the URJ Biennial in Baltimore. At the National Federation of Temple Brotherhoods/Jewish Chautauqua Society booth, the video ran continuously. I was utterly amazed at how many people came up to speak to me and to congratulate me about my appearance in that promotional video. That continued over the course of the next few years at both National and Regional Biennials.

Truly, the JCS made me a star.

I have taught for-credit courses on a number of other college campuses, one of them under the auspices of the JCS. I made a number of appearances at Newbury College, a Lutheran-sponsored college in Newbury, South Carolina, on the one day JCS visitation. The college eventually applied for a JCS grant for a resident lecturer and I was asked to fulfill that responsibility. I gladly accepted but made the mistake of giving myself an impossible day. I drove from Florence, South Carolina, to Laurinburg, North Carolina, to teach at St. Andrews and then drove to Newbury to teach a late afternoon class on that campus. The course was not a success. In my evaluation, I recommended to JCS that the grant could be better utilized at some other institution. I had two reasons for that suggestion. In the first place, the campus chaplain who had initiated the grant proposal was no longer there by the time I began to teach. The new man was not at all supportive and made no significant effort to recommend or publicize the course on campus. Enrollment consisted of approximately fifteen students most of whom were jocks. That was the second problem. None of them were really interested in learning anything from me. None of them really wanted to study, and they certainly were not prepared to write a research paper as part of the course requirement. They were also not interested in attending class or taking a final exam. They were quite interested when they failed. It is the one time in my career where I felt that I was a failure as a teacher.

In addition to these assignments for the JCS, I taught in an extension program for Viterbo College, a Roman Catholic institution in La Crosse, Wisconsin. It held special classes in Wausau for parochial school and church school teachers. These classes were for credit and I taught both my *Introduction to Judaism* program and my *Overview of the Hebrew Bible*. Coker College in Hartsville, South Carolina was a very small privately endowed institution that invited me to teach in their Night School. This was a program for individuals who worked full time and who were interested in obtaining BA or BS degrees in education, sociology, and psychology. They could only take two courses at a time and classes ran for five hours a week for eight weeks. I offered my *Introduction to Judaism* twice. I also taught in their regular day time program for one semester and taught my course on the Hebrew Bible.

Nevertheless, the most unusual teaching that I did occurred in Wausau, Wisconsin. For two years I taught a required course for seniors at Newman High School, which was the local Catholic parochial school. The priest who served as principal was a good friend and we worked together on many community projects. At one point he complained about the fact that so few Catholics knew anything at all about the Judaism out of which their tradition grew. My response was something to the effect that I should then be permitted to teach a course at the high school to give those students the background that he felt they needed. I asked him if he had the courage to try it. His response was, "A turtle only makes progress when it sticks its neck out." Before he could implement the program, he was transferred and a lay person became the new principal.

When he reported for work, he found a file on top of his desk that was labeled important. It described the course that I wanted to teach and urged that it be implemented. He called me into the office early in July and we quickly agreed that I would begin teaching the course in September, that the course would be a requirement, and that it would be offered only to seniors. The course was to be entitled, *The Judaic Background of Christianity.*

In order to smooth the way, I was invited to address all the parents at an opening meeting held about a week before classes started. The principal introduced me and told everyone how pleased he was and how fortunate the school was to have Rabbi Mahrer as a member of its faculty. His praise was effusive and he concluded by saying, "Ladies and gentlemen, please give a warm welcome to Father Mahrer." The error was of course unintentional, but it had the effect of breaking the ice and made my start in that school very comfortable and easy. Only one parent objected to my teaching. He called the principal and said something to the effect that he didn't want his good Catholic son being taught by any g--d--- Jew. The principal promised to call him back. After a quick conversation with the student involved (who was very pleased to be in the class, by the way), he called the parent back with me present in the office. I obviously only heard one side of the conversation, but basically the principal said, "This is a requirement for graduation from our school. Your son is a Senior. The choice is entirely yours. You may withdraw him from school, or you may permit him to continue in a course which he tells me he enjoys." That was the only issue that surrounded the Rabbi teaching in a Catholic parochial high school. As far as I have been able to discover, and I did try, I was the only full-time pulpit Rabbi in the United States ever to have such an assignment.

You need to understand something about me. I am a hugger. I put my arms around the shoulders of my students, whatever grade or class they're in. So, one day after class I was walking through the halls of Newman High School with my arm around a boy on one side and a girl on the other. Three or four other students walked with us as they escorted me to the front door so that I could get in my car to go back to synagogue. Suddenly, one of the teaching Sisters who was in full habit came around the corner and started walking toward us. She exclaimed, "Rabbi, what do you think you're doing?" I responded that I was walking down the hall on my way to my car. She then asked me, "What are you doing with those students?" I told her that I wasn't doing anything with them, but that they were accompanying me to the front door because I was leaving school for the day. She had a very strange look on her face and so I simply said to her, "Come on put your arm around a couple of these kids and you can walk to the front door with us." Unbelievably, she did. When we got to the front door she said, "Rabbi, you are uncontrollable, but I think you are really good for our school and these students." In retrospect that may be the highest praise I have ever received.

Significant Moments: Good, Sad, Even Funny

I have already told you that I was one of the original members of the Human Relations Commission of the City of Battle Creek, Michigan. When I left the community in the spring of 1962, the commissioners of the city of Battle Creek attended the farewell party that the congregation held in my honor. During those festivities they presented me with a framed citation which I keep on the wall of my office. It was one of the proudest moments in my entire career, probably because it came less than three years after my ordination when I certainly did not expect this type of recognition and honor. The citation reads as follows:

Resolution Battle Creek, Michigan, March 27, 1962

Resolved by the Commission of the City of Battle Creek: Whereas Rabbi Lawrence N. Mahrer has served on the Human Relations Commission for the City of Battle Creek from the original organization in 1959, to and including March 27, 1962, fulfilling the post of member of said Commission and later presently Chairman, and

Whereas it is recognized that such civic service as has been performed by Rabbi Mahrer has been time consuming and requires many personal sacrifices

Now therefore, it is hereby resolved, that Rabbi Lawrence N. Mahrer be commended for the time, efficient work and effort that he has extended and performed on behalf of the City of Battle Creek as a member of the Human Relations Commission

It is further resolved, that this resolution be printed on parchment, framed and presented to Rabbi Lawrence N. Mahrer on behalf of the Commissioners and the City of Battle Creek.

Also, early in my career a young woman began to attend services on a very regular basis. From her behavior, it was quite easy to determine that she had never been in a synagogue before, that she did not know exactly how to comport herself, and that she was totally unfamiliar with our rituals and the Hebrew language. However, our congregation had a well-deserved reputation for hospitality and the members made sure that she was comfortable. On a personal basis, I spoke with her at the *Oneg* each *Erev Shabbat*, but our conversations never were very deep. After about two months, I took her aside and initiated a serious conversation that attempted to discover why she was worshipping with us on such a regular basis. She told me that she had been raised in one of the Protestant churches, but eventually came to feel somewhat uncomfortable with many of its teachings about Jesus. During her high school years, she stopped going to church entirely and had not been at any worship service for over ten years before she came to the synagogue. She said that she had picked up a copy of some very simple book, whose title I no longer remember, that was an introduction to Judaism. She decided that she liked what it said. She was attending our service to determine whether she was interested in pursuing the matter any further. I told her that if she decided that she really was interested in going beyond the mere attendance at services on *Erev Shabbat*, she should tell me about it, and we would make a specific appointment to discuss it.

That appointment was made about two months later and we talked about what conversion entailed. I asked her the usual questions about how her family of origin would feel if she became Jewish, etc. I also discovered that she was unmarried and that there was no significant man in her life. I concluded that conversation, as I have always done, by suggesting that she think long and hard about what we had discussed and if she wanted to begin studying with me, she should call me or see me on Friday night and we would begin the process.

That likewise took place. We began studying together for her potential conversion to Judaism.

We met weekly for about an hour and it took probably five or six weeks to discover that much of her conversation was disjointed and that comment number two did not seem to relate very effectively to her first idea. I wondered and thought about it for a while but did nothing. Then, slowly, she began to focus on messianic ideas and concepts. When I tried to tell her that we would discuss that later in our study together, she was quite unhappy and began to insist that we talk about it immediately. Now I was on the verge of becoming alarmed. Furthermore, she became insistent on knowing when our study would be over and when her conversion might take place. That made me even more uncomfortable. Therefore, I arranged for the president of the congregation to be in the synagogue building when she and I were scheduled to have our next session. The synagogue library was immediately outside the door of my office, and when she arrived the president was seated at the table in the library reading (or at least pretending to read) one of our books. He had been told to listen very carefully to the conversation.

After the young woman was seated and we finished the usual small talk, I returned to the subject of messianism and asked her if this had anything to do with why she was so insistent on knowing when her conversion would take place. She assured me that it did. When I asked her for a complete and detailed explanation of the connection between the two, she said to me, "I want to be Jewish as soon as I can be. I am still a virgin. I am going to be the mother of the Messiah and you are going to be his father." Obviously, I told her that would not happen. I told her that she would not be permitted to continue her studies with me and from my point of view she was no longer welcomed to continue to worship with our congregation. The president walked in and told the young woman that he would escort her to the front door of the building. After he let her out, he locked the door and came back to my office to ask me if I had ever experienced anything similar previously. When I told him no, he said, "Well, I certainly hope that you never do in the future either." Thankfully, I never have. I will admit that I have wondered on occasion what it would be like to be the father of the Messiah. I guess I'll never know!

Since we are talking about conversion, I think I will relate another story. One of the young men in the same congregation had been dating a non-Jewish woman all the way through high school and continued into his first year of college. One day the girl and his mother came to see me to ask about conversion. They both said that the kids were planning to get married as soon as it could be arranged and asked if I would be willing to study with this young lady for her conversion to Judaism. Since she was still living at home, I told her that I would be happy to discuss it with her, but that I would like her to bring her parents to see me so that I could be certain that they had no real objection. She told me that wouldn't be necessary and asked if she could use the phone. She called home and when her mother answered she told her mother that I wanted to talk with her. And so, I did. I was told that there was no objection at all to the daughter becoming Jewish and that the family was looking forward, enthusiastically, to the wedding. When that phone conversation ended, I scheduled an appointment with the young girl and told her that we would begin immediately. A couple of months into our study together, she was again accompanied to my office by her future mother-in-law. They both told me that the girl was pregnant and that was the cause for the rush on the wedding. They assured me that these kids had intended to be married eventually, which I already knew. They knew that I did not perform interreligious marriages and that that was the reason for the conversion at this time. However, they indicated that the pregnancy was beginning to show because the girl was so slim, and they were concerned about having the wedding as soon as possible.

I asked what was the earliest date that they could plan for the wedding and I agreed to conduct the wedding on that date even though her conversion would not be complete. I made it very clear to both that I expected her to come back to my community once a week after she had moved into an apartment with her new husband until the conversion was completed. She readily agreed to do that, and we continued. Unfortunately, when I violated my principals about an interreligious marriage, I made a huge mistake.

The wedding took place approximately a month later and she continued to study with me for another ten weeks or so. Then we held the conversion ceremony.

A healthy son was born, and I went to the college town in which they were living, accompanied by both sides of the family, to officiate at the *Brit Milah*. I left the congregation approximately six months later.

Imagine my surprise when, in a phone conversation with a former congregant, I was informed that after the child's first birthday his mother took him to her former church where he was baptized and christened, and that she and her son were at church almost every Sunday morning. There was a Christmas tree in the home and nothing Jewish. It certainly was clear to me that she had used me and the pretense of conversion to get married and satisfy her husband's family. Many years later, when this child was around nine years old, I was asked to return to the community to conduct a funeral for the husband's grandmother who had been a very special friend of mine. When I was introduced to the boy at whose circumcision I had officiated, he said something about the fact that I had a funny first name. I asked him what he meant, and he said that he knew a lot of people, but he had never met anybody named "Rabbi." This boy, who as an eight-day old infant had been circumcised and given a Hebrew name and welcomed into the covenant of Abraham our father, was so lacking in knowledge and so totally divorced from anything Jewish that he had never heard the word Rabbi before.

I bent my rules and violated my principles by performing that marriage prior to conversion. I really felt used by that young woman and vowed that I would never make the same mistake again. I have not.

As I have written previously, during my first two years in Peoria, I covered two assignments for Moses Montefiore Congregation in Bloomington so they would continue to be available when they had full time rabbinic service again. One of those was to serve as the part time Jewish chaplain for the Lincoln State School. This facility was for the severely mentally handicapped who could not be cared for at home. Each visit consisted of my conducting a brief service of worship using a booklet that had been prepared by one of Bloomington's earlier rabbis. It had been used for many years and the residents of the school had memorized everything in it. The school supplied us with a piano player, and we sang some Hebrew responses and a couple of English songs. Because the men and women who attended this service had memorized it, they all clamored for the opportunity to come and stand in front of the group to recite a paragraph. It was interesting to watch them show off what they had remembered and to see the smiles of pride and pleasure on their faces as they resumed their seats. This was an interesting time for me, because it was my first real exposure to individuals with significant intellectual disabilities. They were wonderful, but it was so sad that it was necessary for them to be institutionalized.

The Lincoln State School was the location of one of the most touching experiences in my rabbinate. I was called to come to the school for a funeral and entered the large gymnasium to find it almost filled with men and women. The casket was in the front of the room and there was a lectern that had been provided for me. I was introduced by the full-time chaplain, who reminded everyone how serious a funeral was, and then I began. I had rewritten much that was in the *Rabbi's Manual* to language that was quite simple and I condensed the service to about ten minutes. When I concluded, the chaplain took my place at the lectern and told everybody that it was now time to say goodbye. Obviously, the people in attendance knew exactly what he meant, because they began to line up along the wall of the room. While they were doing that, the top half of the lid of the casket was opened so that the deceased's head and shoulders were exposed. Without any further prompting, the residents of the school came forward to say goodbye. Some stopped to look. Others, to say goodbye. Some reached into the casket to touch and a few bent over and kissed the body of the young man. Not one sound was spoken as maybe 150 people walked by that casket. I was truly moved and have spoken about that experience many times. The casket was driven to Chicago that same day for a funeral attended by family members and friends and burial in a Jewish cemetery in the Chicago area.

On another occasion I was called to conduct a funeral and this time was told to go to the cemetery and park my car under the beautiful trees that lined the drive. I arrived five to ten minutes before the scheduled time and saw a freshly opened grave about 100 feet from the trees. A truck was parked nearby. As I walked toward the grave, the driver of the truck came out to meet me and said, "You da preach?" When I informed him that I was the Rabbi for the funeral, he motioned to the truck and three other men got out. The four of them took the casket off the back of the truck and lowered it into the grave and quickly got into the truck and drove away. So, I was left alone in the middle of the cemetery, standing next to an open grave with a casket in it. I stood around for a while, waiting to see if anybody was going to arrive. When it was ten minutes past the scheduled time, I simply recited the 23rd Psalm, one of the meditations from the *Rabbi's Manual* and said *Kaddish*. By the time I got back to my car, the truck had returned to the grave and the four men were busily filling it in with shovels.

On my way out of the grounds, I stopped at the chaplain's office to find out what had happened. I was told that the deceased was a man approximately 80 years old who had been living in the hospital for over a dozen years. There was no family of record and because he was so old and had been isolated in the hospital for so long, no one knew him. One funeral experience at the Lincoln State School was touching and uplifting and the other was mournful and devastating.

Interviews are another interesting aspect of the life of a Rabbi. On one occasion I was met at the airport and driven to the community in which the synagogue was located. I was given time to freshen up and relax a little in my hotel room and then was picked up for dinner with the search committee. We arrived at the private room in the restaurant and found a long table and about a dozen people. I was individually introduced to each and then the waitress came in and asked us for our drink order. As she brought our drinks, she put menus at each place at the table and after we stood around for a little bit talking and drinking, someone suggested that we sit down and look at the menus. We did. Then the waitress came back and asked if anybody wanted another drink and many of us did. But she never asked us if we were ready to order. I finally turned to the chairman of the committee who was sitting alongside me and suggested that if he didn't want me to be completely drunk and inarticulate, we ought to get along with the eating part of the evening. He kind of smiled sheepishly and said, "Well, we are waiting for you." I noticed that he and others who had overheard the conversation appeared to be somewhat embarrassed, but I never caught on. Finally, I asked and said, "What is this all about?" It turned out that they were waiting for me to say something about what I was going to eat so that they could have some clue as to whether it would be proper to order seafood and other non-Kosher items. I stood up and said, "Ladies and gentlemen I am much more interested in what comes out of your mouth than what goes into it. Let's relax, eat and enjoy." By the way, I got the job.

When Rabbi Malcolm Stern was the Director of the Placement Commission of the CCAR and the URJ, he arranged consecutive interviews for me. One was in New Jersey near Newark and the other was on Long Island. I was very impressed with the people and the congregation in New Jersey and I was offered the pulpit. However, I was not at all certain that I wanted a congregation that large or that I wanted a congregation that was really part of the New York Metroplex. I had spent all my life until then in the northern Midwest in small congregations. I told all of that to the folks in New Jersey before I went on to my second interview. The chairman of the search committee, who later assumed major leadership roles in the URJ, even came to visit the community in which I was serving to convince me to accept his congregation's offer.

When I left that town, I went into Manhattan and spent some time in the CCAR office with Malcolm. He asked me one question. "Do you want to see your name up in lights?" My negative response convinced me that I really did not want to become the rabbi of that congregation. The man who did assume that pulpit went on to an illustrious and very prominent career. His is a rabbinate for which I know I was not, and am still not, suited.

After leaving Malcolm's office, I took the train out to Long Island. I was met at the station, driven around the community briefly, and then taken to the synagogue. It was a converted two-story house onto which a combination sanctuary and Social Hall had been added. I got there on a Thursday afternoon and the building was filthy from its use the previous weekend. Wastebaskets were overflowing, tables and chairs were strewn around all the rooms, dirty dishes were still on the counters and in the sinks in the kitchen, blackboards had not been washed in the classrooms, and none of the lavatories had been cleaned. I was very surprised at what I saw, particularly since they knew I was arriving. I expected a "best foot forward" effort.

Then I was taken to a private home where I was supposed to spend the night. When the committee chairman stopped the car in front of the home, I reminded him that he and I had agreed over the phone that I would be spending the night in a motel because I desired my privacy. His response was that it couldn't be arranged. I was introduced to the woman of the family, shown to a bedroom in the back, given some towels, and had the door to the room closed as she left. I never saw her again until about 7:45 when I was picked up for the 8:00 interview meeting. For the third time in my career, I went without dinner. When the chairman and I arrived at the synagogue, several other people were hurriedly trying to clean up and straighten up a room so that we could hold a meeting in it. The meeting began with everyone telling me how proud they were of their congregation and of their synagogue.

After about 15 to 20 minutes of listening to these people rave about their congregation and congratulate themselves about their wonderful facility, I asked the president if he would come out into the hall to speak with me privately for a moment. When he did, I suggested that we do everybody a favor by simply telling the committee that I was no longer interested in being their rabbi, and that it probably would be better for everyone if we all went home. I asked him if he would drive me back to the house where I was staying so that I could explain this to him in more detail. When we returned to the room, he very kindly and graciously explained my feelings to the committee, thanked me for coming, and thanked them for taking the time out of their busy lives to be present that night.

In his car on the way home I told him that I had been assured that I would be staying in a motel and not in a private home, that I had anticipated being invited out to dinner, and that I was very surprised that they had brought a rabbinic candidate into their building without first making certain that the building was at least presentable, if not clean. Since no one on the committee seemed to feel that there was anything wrong with the building, or with the way I had been treated, I told him that I knew I just wouldn't fit in. As he dropped me off, I suggested that he pick me up in the morning, take me to breakfast, and then drop me off at the train station. He agreed. He picked me up and took me to the train station, but he forgot about breakfast. When I got back to the airport in Newark, I had my first meal in over 24 hours.

The rabbi that they did bring to occupy that pulpit stayed with them for approximately two years. Shortly after he left, he wrote a scathing book about how difficult it had been for him to be the rabbi of that congregation. He described the difference between his value system and the value system of the members of that community and congregation and how totally unhappy he and his family had been in that position. I guess I wasn't wrong.

What I found interesting about the interview process is the fact that at no time was I ever asked any questions about my own personal belief system, value system, or theology. This caused me some difficulty. All the matters that I discussed with various search committees and boards were practical: how would I run the Religious School, how do I feel about interfaith relations, will

I or won't I perform an interreligious marriage and so forth. No one ever wanted to know who I really was.

In 1949, the renowned newspaper and television reporter, Edward R. Murrow started a 15-minute radio program in which he asked individuals to state their personal philosophy of life and their value system. It likewise became a newspaper column. It was called, *This I Believe*, and became one of the most listened to radio programs of all time and one of the most widely syndicated newspaper columns in the world. It was published in book form in 1952 by Simon and Schuster. I listened to that radio program and I read those articles in the Cleveland Press. Eventually I found a copy of the book in a used book store in Cincinnati. I recommend it to everybody.

When I began to discover that the search committees of the congregations which I eventually served never asked me about my personal belief system and never really attempted to discover who I was at my core, I determined to use the first set of High Holiday sermons in each new congregation to introduce myself to my congregants at this level. I began the practice in 1966 with my congregation in Peoria, Illinois, and have used it in six subsequent pulpits.

In one of those congregations, I had a letter of agreement signed by both myself and the president which, among other things, stated that I would serve as the rabbi for three years. After I delivered two of these *This, I Believe* sermons on *Rosh HaShanah*, there was an emergency board meeting. One of the very wealthy men in the congregation told the president that I could not be his rabbi because my ideas, value system, and beliefs did not coincide with his own. I knew nothing about any of this until about four weeks later when I received a formal contract from the board. Much to my surprise it was for two years instead of three. When I asked, I was told the story. I then asked how often this individual came to service. It was indicated to me that he attended services for the High Holidays and maybe two or three times on *Shabbat* during the rest of the year. I found it fascinating that a congregant who was basically a nonparticipant could cause a congregation to violate its agreement with its rabbi. I told the board that I was unable to sign their contract because it violated the letter of agreement that we had already signed and that I refused to subject myself to the pressures generated by a large donor. I also informed the board that I would be leaving as soon as I could find another pulpit. I stayed slightly less than two years.

When my middle child, Jeff, was in high school in the suburbs of St. Louis, he became a member of the Speech Team. He was looking for something humorous that he could read in the various competitions. I gave him a novel by Herbert Tarr entitled, *Heaven Help Us!* Tarr was a rabbi and ordained by HUC-JIR in 1955. He was a military chaplain, a pulpit rabbi, and a novelist. *Heaven Help Us!* was published in 1968 by Random House.

The section that Jeffrey chose to use came at the very beginning of the book and describes the rabbi's interview at a nameless congregation. It goes on for a few pages and it is, from my point of view, hysterically funny. A small part of it reads as follows:

A longer silence this time, only now I welcomed it as a respite from questions. These were my people here, so tell me, why were they persecuting me?

"Rabbi? How do you feel about the State of Israel?"

This was like my first date all over again, when the girl asking anything that came to mind and my chattering away because we both fearfully regarded silence as something that existed only to be clogged, like a sewer. "Well, even before reading *Exodus*..."

I haven't said anything, had I? Yet all of a sudden the Trustees began to chant, *"Exodus! Exodus! Exodus!"* It was so soul-warming, eliciting a response at last, that when the roar abated, I couldn't resist starting it up again. "Yes, even before *Exodus*..."

They were off, *"Exodus! Exodus! Exodus!"* they exclaimed, as in "Two-four-six-eight, who do we appreciate?"

I have been to interviews like that. However, my favorite interview was in Dothan, Alabama. I met with the Board of Trustees for about an hour. I then conducted a very brief service of worship for many congregants who had come to the synagogue and then we moved into the Social Hall where congregants were given the opportunity to ask me questions. After about thirty minutes of that, a six-year-old by the name of Benjamin Wells raised his hand. I called on him and wondered what was about to happen.

In a very soft voice he said, "I'd like to have you as our Rabbi." I walked closer to him, asked him to stand up on his chair, which he did, and then I said, "Benjamin. Say that again, very loud!" He did. Everyone laughed. I felt terrific. I got the job. He is still my friend.

My in-laws lived the last 25 years of their lives in Hollywood, Florida. They were members of Temple Beth El, and for most of those years Rabbi Samuel Jaffee served that congregation. My family attended services with them whenever we visited on a Friday night, because my in-laws never let anything interfere with their participation in services on *Erev Shabbat*. In the late 1960s, on one of our visits, we all went to the Temple for services. As I approached the door, I took my *kipah* and placed it on my head. At the entrance to the Sanctuary, the usher stopped me and said, "I'm sorry, but we don't do that." I asked him what it was that they didn't do? He told me that they did not permit men to worship with a head covering. I responded, "Will you do me a favor? Will you tell Rabbi Jaffee that you asked Rabbi Mahrer to remove his head covering?" In a very embarrassed way, the man began to apologize to me and indicated that he didn't know that I was a rabbi and, of course, I could continue to keep my head covered. I then said, "Are you telling me that it is OK for a rabbi to wear a *kipah* in your sanctuary but that it isn't OK for Joe Jew? That's an interesting distinction." At that point, I simply sat down with the family. My father-in-law later told me that beginning with the next *Erev Shabbat*, he always wore a *kipah* to services. He said that my question about 'Joe Jew' made him realize how foolish the congregation's rules were.

On another occasion, probably in the middle 1970s, my son Scott came to services with us. He was in his young teenage years. It was in the summer and he was very nicely dressed wearing clean, pressed slacks and a short-sleeved dress shirt. This time he was the one stopped by the usher (a different one) and told that he could not enter the sanctuary without a jacket. He turned to his grandfather and asked for the keys to the car. He said that he would simply sit in the parking lot and listen to the radio until the service was over. The usher told him that would not be necessary because they had jackets available for people to wear. When Scott began to get angry, I gave him a little hand signal and nodded and suggested that he do what the usher requested. By this time everybody else in the family had been seated and while the usher was off getting a jacket for Scott. I said, "Scott, we're going to stay here in the hallway until immediately before the beginning of services, and then I want you to follow me into the sanctuary and do exactly what I do." The usher returned with an ill-fitting, ugly green jacket which Scott put on. We just lingered in the hallway outside the sanctuary until it was time to begin. At that point we walked into the sanctuary, down the center aisle with me leading the way. When we got to the second row from the front, where the family always sat, I very slowly and ostentatiously removed my jacket and my tie and draped them over the end of the pew. Scott did likewise and we were seated with the family with no further incident. By the way, at the end of the service, Scott left the congregation's jacket in the pew.

At the exact opposite end of the spectrum from the hassling of my son, Scott, I remember a rabbi in Wheeling, West Virginia, in the 1950s and 1960s who had a completely different approach. I don't know whether what I am about to describe happened every Friday night or on some other kind of schedule. He invited his teenagers to a service intended exclusively for them, about an hour earlier than the regular adult service, so that they could participate in *Shabbat* and still have time for all their normal, Friday night teenage activities. Additionally, he told the kids to wear the clothing that they were going to wear for the rest of the night, whether it was jeans, shorts, or fancy party/dance clothing. While I never attended one of those services, I did have contact with some of the kids who did and was told that they were well attended, a big hit, and appreciated both by the kids and their parents.

I remember riding in my car on a weekend afternoon in central Illinois while I was relaxing and taking in the sights. On the radio, I heard some sort of news program in which it was reported that Stokley Carmichael had created the slogan, "Black Is

Beautiful." I was impressed. Long before I had any idea as to the effect of that phrase on the black community, I absolutely knew that we needed something similar for Jews and Judaism. It didn't take me very long, maybe a matter of months, to create the phrase, "Jewish Is Joyous."

Not only did I create a slogan, but I captured what I truly believed to be a significant aspect of the essence of our tradition. Maybe, I am a *Chassid* masquerading in the garb of a Reform Rabbi. Nonetheless, I had always been concerned about the intense emphasis on decorum, quietness, order and synchronized praying which was so evident in the Reform congregations of my youth and my early rabbinic career.

The slogan helped me learn to loosen up and I began to encourage my congregants to speak out during sermons so that they could react to what I said. Later, as I introduced the silent prayer at the end of the *Amidah*, I began to say, "Is there anyone in the sanctuary this evening who would like to say something out loud to the rest of us?" In each new congregation it took people a long time to realize that I was serious in my request, and then, slowly people began to respond. Individuals would say something about a *Simchah* in their family or an illness in the family or among the congregants, or make a comment about something that was in the news. On average, I would get a response to that request approximately every other week.

I remember one occasion in a previous synagogue where one of the doctors came into services somewhat late. In response to my question, he made a comment about the fact that he had just come from the hospital where he had delivered a baby. Neither mother nor child were doing as well as expected and he asked us to keep them in our thoughts. The following Friday night, he reminded us of what he had said the previous week and told us that both mother and child were doing very well and that they had gone home the previous day.

Miscellaneous Mishugas

Early in 1960, someone who was not a member of the congregation in Battle Creek came to me and said that he had heard that I worked well with teenagers. He wondered whether I would be willing to serve as the chaplain to the Civil Air Patrol, with emphasis on dealing with their teenage cadets. After I discovered what was involved, I readily agreed. Working with teenagers, none of whom were Jewish, and dealing with issues of morality, ethics, and citizenship proved to be quite a challenge, because our frame of reference was somewhat different. I really enjoyed that opportunity and those kids. It also gave me the chance to do some flying as a passenger.

Battle Creek is of course the headquarters of the Kellogg's company, and Post cereals had a large plant there as well. Every spring, the city hosted the Cereal City Festival, which featured "the longest breakfast table in the world." By borrowing tables and chairs from schools, congregations, clubs, and other facilities, the city was able to stretch out a breakfast table down the main street for many, many blocks. Kellogg's and Post donated little boxes of cereal, dairies donated small containers of milk, bakeries donated donuts and other pastries, and grocery stores donated orange juice and sugar. Literally thousands of people came to eat breakfast on a Saturday morning. When that was over, it was followed by an extended parade down the same street.

In the spring of 1961, someone arranged for a bicycle road race from Detroit to Battle Creek. The finish line was in the middle of the main street and it was estimated that the race would end during breakfast. The Civil Air Patrol owned a small airplane and I was asked if I would ride along with the pilot so that I could broadcast the progress of the race back to the radio station, which would announce it on loudspeakers out to the street. I had three minutes on the hour and on the half hour. When friends found out what I was doing, many of them gave me cameras so that I could take pictures as we flew alongside and over the bicycle racers. I took my 8mm movie camera with a telephoto lens for my own purposes.

Just before we left the airport, the pilot checked with the state police and found out exactly where the lead riders were, and we took off to find them. That wasn't particularly difficult, and since we had some time before my first radio report was scheduled, we simply flew alongside the bicycles at what was most likely an illegally low altitude. The pilot kept the wings tilted toward the riders so that I could take photographs through the window.

When we got to the first rider in line, the pilot spun the plane 180 degrees so that we could go back up the other side, and I got somewhat queasy. We got back up to a normal altitude and the pilot read off the numbers on the backs of the riders and told me where we were located on the highway and I made my first report. I did two more of them and continued to take pictures between reports. . I never realized how unsettling it was to look through a viewfinder on a camera and focus on things moving on the ground while moving in an airplane. Needless to say, I eventually threw up all over the inside of the plane.

After I finished my third radio report, we returned to the airport. When the pilot taxied the plane to its permanent location, he opened the door, got out, and said, "I'll tie the plane down, refuel it and check the oil. You know the rules. The CAP plane must be ready to be used on a moment's notice. I'm sorry, but you'll have to clean up the mess inside." With a significant lack of enthusiasm, I found a bucket, some rags, and some water. What I remember specifically is my pleasure in knowing that I would not be the next person to have to fly in that plane.

Some of those photographs and some of my movies turned out fairly well. I also had a whole series of movies of my kids growing up and our days at the URJ camp in Wisconsin. My son Scott has edited them all together, given them titles, and put them on DVD. Most of the family even managed to do a voice over on those two long videos. I still watch them occasionally with a great deal of pleasure.

The movies from our days at camp have been uploaded by Scott to the OSRUI Alumni page on Facebook. They have been viewed and commented upon many times, which pleases me to no end. They have also become part of the American Jewish Archives at HUC-JIR.

Jane Chapnan was a member of our congregation in Florence, South Carolina, and taught in our Religious School. One Sunday, at the end of classes, I stopped her in the Social Hall and asked if we could talk for a couple of minutes. She told me she was in a bit of a hurry but since I had said a couple of minutes, she agreed. She asked her young daughter named Laura who was about five or six years old to call home and tell Daddy that she and Mom would be delayed for a few minutes. As she skipped off towards the kitchen to find a phone, Jane and I began our conversation. Suddenly there was a very soft, plaintiff voice from the kitchen which said, "Mom, how do you use this telephone?" That's when Jane and I realized how times had changed, that technology had taken over our lives, and young Laura could not use an old-style rotary telephone.

Here's another story about another young girl, whose name will be changed because her real name is too recognizable. I think I'll call her Margie. Somewhere around the age of ten, while Margie was a student in a private school, she participated in a daylong series of athletic events called field day. Her mother, who was an active volunteer for the school, was there all day as well. When mom took Margie home, the ten-year-old complained of being very stiff and sore. So, mom put her in a nice, warm bath to relax for a while and found the family's barbershop type vibrator. That's the kind where the barber put the machine on the back of his hand and it vibrated his fingers sufficiently so that he could give an excellent scalp massage. I haven't seen one of those used in 25 years or more. Nonetheless, Mom found it, and after Margie was dried and stretched out on the bed, Mom gave her a thorough massage on her neck, her arms, her back and her legs.

Because of the mother's activity level in the community, she wore a pager attached to the outside of her purse. The following afternoon, while she was in the midst of a meeting of some community committee on which she served, the pager went off and the voice said, "Mom! This is Margie. Where did you put the vibrator? I want to use it." That was, I am told, the last day that mother wore the pager.

About six years later, the mother was a teacher in our Religious School and Margie came to see me a minute or two before school ended. She was already driving her own sports car. We stood talking in the Social Hall and she asked me if I thought that she should have her nose fixed. I certainly wasn't going to answer that question either way, because no matter what I said I would be wrong, or somebody would be upset. So, I simply asked her what the doctor had recommended. She told me that the doctor had said that the decision was entirely up to her and that, if her present nose made her feel uncomfortable or unattractive, she might want to have cosmetic surgery. But, in any case, he told her she was still growing and the surgery would have to wait about another year or year and a half. The conversation continued for a little while and Margie was unaware of the fact that her mother had walked up directly behind her. Margie concluded the conversation by saying to me, "Yes. I think I'll do it. I'm pretty sure that I'm gonna get my nose fixed and my boobs made bigger, just the way Mom did." Mom turned a variety of colors of red, before turning and quietly walking out of the Social Hall. Margie thanked me for listening, left the building, and drove off. Her mother came out of the back hallway and looked me right in the eye and said, "I don't know whether to laugh, to lie down and die or what. In any case I am mortified." I really wanted to ask her whether Margie had told the truth about her nose and the other parts of her anatomy, but I thought better of it. Margie grew up to be an attorney.

I was invited to officiate at the wedding of one of my female cousins. Her older sister was the matron of honor. About halfway through the ceremony, the bride began to cry. I reached into my jacket pocket and took out the clean handkerchief which I always kept for such emergencies. I put it in the palm of my hand and held it out toward the matron of honor. She promptly blinked and one of her blue-tinted contact lenses fell directly into it. The bride's tears changed to laughter and the marriage ceremony was a huge success.

Many years earlier, I had been asked to co-officiate at the wedding of one of the members of the staff of the URJ camp in Wisconsin. Since I was fond of both the bride and the groom, I was very pleased to accept. Another Rabbi from the camp faculty was also involved, but the chief officiant was the traditional rabbi from the bride's hometown. Before the ceremony, the men were gathered in the rabbi's study. He suddenly took me, my colleague, and the groom out of the room and down the Religious School hall to a classroom which was being used as the dressing room for the bride. He knocked on the door and we were invited in. The bride was already veiled, and he led the groom to within inches of the bride, lifted the veil and said, "Is this the right one?" When he was assured that it was, he led us out of the room and back to his office. That was an aspect of Jewish wedding which I had never experienced previously, but my knowledge indicated that it must have had something to do with Jacob and the biblical story of his marriage to Leah instead of to Rachel, the woman whom he loved. When we got back to the study, the rabbi explained all of this, in very patient detail, to us less than kosher co-officiants.

During the ceremony itself, when he asked the best man for the ring, he held it out first to me and then to the other Reform Rabbi. In both instances he asked us something in Yiddish which I certainly did not understand and which I discovered the other Reform Rabbi didn't understand either. At the reception which followed, somebody asked me what I had replied when the Rabbi asked me, "Is this valuable enough?" In other words, he asked us whether the ring was of sufficient value to be used to "secure" the bride. Clearly, he took our silence for assent.

At the very end of the wedding, he got caught. However carefully things had been arranged under the *Chuppah*, someone had forgotten to place a piece of glass on the table to be broken by the groom. Seeing this omission, the rabbi removed his watch and laid it on the floor, glass crystal side up. The groom gave him the most puzzled look imaginable, and when the rabbi nodded affirmatively, the groom tromped on it.

At every wedding that I have conducted, somebody asks whether I can keep the ceremony short. Long after I have left the pulpit in Kenosha, Wisconsin, I was invited back to conduct the marriage ceremony of the daughter of some very close friends. The wedding was to be held in the family's backyard, in the open, with the rest of the yard taken up with a huge tent for the reception. The sky was a magnificent, Wisconsin azure blue (which can only be believed after it has been seen). Unusually, the temperature was in the mid-nineties. We all gathered in the somewhat air-conditioned house until it was time for the ceremony to begin. The guests then made their way into the yard to sit on the metal folding chairs which had been exposed to the sun for three or four hours. They, more than the rest of us, were very uncomfortable. When the bride and groom took their place in front of me, she said, "I know everybody asks. You told us so. Just this once, can you do this quickly?" Frankly, I had not planned to, but when one of the bridesmaids fainted, I figured it was time to be both brief and hurried. I am sure I will never forget the sweaty dampness of that wedding. Bob Alper, my comedian colleague, uses a similar story in his routine. It is only funny because it is true.

Memorable Moments in an Ordinary Rabbinate

It began on a Sunday between *Rosh HaShanah* and *Yom Kippur* in 1987. It happened in the congregation's cemetery following the traditional memorial service held between the holidays. Tom Grossman, a Holocaust survivor, came up to me and said, "It's right that we should come to the cemetery to remember family members and others who contributed so much to our lives. But it would also be right for us to remember the victims of the *Shoah*. We need a memorial for them right here."

Over the next couple of weeks, we talked about his idea and we went to the company that created most of the headstones for our Jewish community and shared our thoughts. They designed a memorial which was basically a ten-foot-tall pillar of granite planted in a bed of gray gravel, surrounded by a low granite wall and with pillars at each corner joined together by black chain. They explained their symbolism of the gray gravel as representing the ashes of Jews who were cremated and the wall, pillars, and chain representing the concentration camps. The tall narrow granite monument, in their conception, represented the Jewish community still reaching upward toward God.

We accepted their design and talked with a few others from the synagogue to come up with the words and the symbols that would be etched into the front of the granite pillar. When everything was done, we were given a price to have it made and installed on the grounds of the cemetery. Then, Tom and I began to call on congregants in order to raise the money that would be necessary. Two or three of those people said that the monument belonged in front of the synagogue where it could be seen on a regular basis, rather than tucked away in a relatively remote and obscure cemetery. Tom and I brought that idea to the Board of Trustees, and much to my surprise and pleasure, they readily agreed. The fundraising was easy, and the monument was in place ready to be dedicated at the congregation's observance of *Yom HaShoah* the following spring.

Each year thereafter, as long as I continued to serve Beth Israel Congregation, the community was invited to observe *Yom HaShoah* with the congregation. We never had fewer than 150 people present, no matter what day of the week on which the observance fell. Various friends of mine from the Christian clergy participated in the service and our main speaker was always a prominent person including our governor, one of our state senators, and the congressman who represented our district in Washington. Media attention to this event was always excellent prior to, during, and after the observance. I truly feel that this monument became the focal point for a significant community education endeavor regarding the Holocaust.

Many years previously, I created another annual event which focused on education, understanding, and acceptance. Years earlier, I remember reading an article by Maurice "Maurie" Davis, about whom I have already written, which I think was published in the *National Jewish Post and Opinion*. As I remember it, Maurie suggested that we needed a Hate Week to replace Brotherhood Week. The concept was that if we would hate each other one week out of the year, it should be possible for us to love each other for the rest of the year.

I always observed Brotherhood Week in my synagogues in the typical way by sharing the pulpit with a Christian colleague. Occasionally, I would be asked to share his pulpit the following Sunday. While initially the activity created a "feel good" impression, it had no significant result. My dissatisfaction led to my creating Neighbor Night that was held on the *Erev Shabbat* of Brotherhood Week.

The idea was for my congregants to invite their non-Jewish neighbors, friends, business associates, and others to worship with us that evening. The service would be shortened somewhat so that it could be thoroughly explained as it was conducted. Additionally, in place of a sermon, our guests would be permitted to ask questions about any aspect of Jewish life in which they were interested. An extra special *Oneg Shabbat* always followed the service. In each congregation that I served, it took a couple of years for the idea to catch on with congregants. At first, they appeared hesitant to invite their friends to the synagogue for such an experience. Eventually, however, it became highly successful. Frequently guests who had attended asked their hosts for permission to come back again. If you remember, the students whom I taught at St. Andrews Presbyterian College as a JCS Resident Lecturer were always invited to attend this service.

I'm certain that every rabbi who serves in a congregation has many Christian groups that come to the synagogue for an explanation of Judaism, the synagogue, our rituals, and so forth. Each pulpit rabbi could create a list of the five to ten most asked questions, and I know that most of them would appear on almost all the lists. I had a very interesting experience during one of these sessions many years ago, when a group of high school students from a church came to meet with me at the synagogue early one Sunday evening. My procedure was to quickly show our guests around the sanctuary pointing out the *Ner Tamid*, the *menorot*, the Ten Commandments, the Ark, and the scrolls of *Torah*. Then, I showed them the various components of our worship service by having them page through the *siddur*. At the end, when I talked about *Kaddish*, I pointed out the *Yahrzeit* tablets on the wall of the sanctuary. I always had a few of the lights lit. When it became time for their questions, most of the time I found that some of the questions focused on our ideas of life after death.

When that question came, I suggested to the group that we pick up the prayer book one more time and look at the content of some of the meditations that precede the *Kaddish*. I pointed out that they talk about memory, about the immortality of the human soul, but that they never refer to heaven or hell. On this one occasion, as I indicated that we don't believe in a heaven, one teenage girl blurted out, "Then why be good?" No sooner had she said it than she began to apologize for her interruption. I assured her that it was not an interruption and that it was a very legitimate question. Nonetheless, she felt badly about her lack of self-control.

I asked her and the others in the group what is the reason for a human to be good. Most of the responses dealt with the idea of being able to merit going to heaven. When I suggested that Judaism's concept is that a person should be good and behave properly simply because it was the right thing to do, without any thought about a potential reward, it appeared as if I had presented them with an entirely new idea. I was fascinated as I watched, listened, and somewhat participated for the next ten or fifteen minutes as this group of high school students struggled with the idea that one should behave properly simply because it was right.

Early in the fall of 1968, the conductor of the Peoria Symphony Orchestra named Dr. Harold Bauer asked me if I would help him prepare for the *King David Oratorio*. This was a Symphonic Psalm written by Arthur Honegger and the orchestra was going to present it with the Bradley University Community

Chorus. He was a little bit disturbed by the language of the narration because so much of it, particularly portions quoted from the Bible, were so stilted in their style. I agreed, and we immediately set about rewriting a good bit of it. When we finished many weeks later, he asked me if we could go into the synagogue's sanctuary so that I could read the narration aloud to him while he got a feel for it. When that was over, he asked me if I would be willing to narrate the actual performance. Again, I agreed! Maybe it's important for you to know that Dr. Bauer was Jewish, but not involved with our Jewish community.

It was absolutely amazing to me to discover how difficult it was to put together such a production. It was a 70-piece orchestra, chorus of 133 voices, five soloists, and me as the narrator. Two aspects of it were particularly hard for me. While I can read music and have no real problem following a piano piece, I never had the opportunity to look at, much less attempt to follow, a symphonic score. That is hard. I stood next to the harpist who helped me know when to start talking. Furthermore, wearing a tuxedo added difficulty for this ordinarily casually dressed man. The review in the Peoria Journal Star ran on Wednesday, January 22, 1969. It had these two sentences in it: "...conductor Harold Bauer not only put it all together with apparent ease, but made a smashing show out of it." It also said, "Rabbi Maher's articulate, poetic narration, helped breathe life into the story of David from his days as a shepherd to the crowning of Solomon and the death of the King." I have spoken in public thousands of times, but this is the only time I have ever been reviewed in print. Goodness knows, congregants reviewed me every week.

At a CCAR convention somewhere in the middle 1980s, I was presented with an award from the Conference for having given 20 years of my rabbinate to the service of small congregations. My guess is that most young rabbis, at the time of ordination, have some sort of dream or plan for how they would like their careers to work out. Based on what I saw as the success of Maurie Davis in his career, I visited him at his pulpit named Indianapolis Hebrew Congregation to talk with him about my goals. I went just before my ordination. My primary question was whether I should consider being someone's assistant or occupy a small solo pulpit. He responded very quickly with a comment to the effect that my personality would make it difficult for me to be someone's assistant. I understood exactly what he was talking about and so, when the placement process began, I only expressed interest in small congregations.

About twelve or fifteen years after ordination, my dream was to have a congregation between 350 and 400 families. I would be immensely happy and set for life. To some extent my plans worked out. I assumed the pulpit in Battle Creek with approximately 50 families, then moved to Kenosha with about 100 families. It was then on to Peoria with about 200 families. Thirteen years after ordination I was in St. Louis with a congregation of approximately 380 families. That placement was supposed to be an extremely happy, lifetime marriage. It wasn't and ended in divorce about 17 months later. After ending that, I was out of the pulpit rabbinate for three and a half years. For the first year and a half I attended the University of Missouri - St.

Louis and picked up a Master's Degree in Education. I then tried, with very limited success, to be a camp director. I ended up working for a Jewish bookstore in Chicago for two years while I served the congregation in Oshkosh, Wisconsin on the weekends. I also taught in the Religious Schools and the adult education programs of several congregations in the Chicago area. In 1977 I had the opportunity to return to the congregational rabbinate and have subsequently served only small congregations. It was a very wise, conscious choice and I was truly happy with almost every aspect of the last 25 plus years of my rabbinic career.

It pleased me that the CCAR and its committee on the rabbinate in small communities recognized the choice I made and the things I accomplished. They presented me with an award for twenty plus years of service to small congregations. The presentation was held at a daylong seminar for rabbis of small congregations and was the day before a national convention. As I said, I was pleased to receive this recognition. However, during the National CCAR convention itself that very same year, there was a very prominent place on the program for the presentation of awards to rabbis who had served in the military chaplaincy for twenty years. Immediately following that presentation, I returned my award to the Executive Vice President of the CCAR. The disparity between the presentation at the fall national convention to military chaplains and the presentation to me in a room with approximately ten people clearly indicated that the CCAR still was not concerned with rabbis who had elected to spend their career serving in small congregations.

This involvement with small congregations eventually made it possible for me to be one of the first members of the URJ Small Congregations Committee. It worked in conjunction with the Small Congregations Department of the Union and was directed by my friend and colleague Norman Kahan. This work led to the development of many long-lasting friendships and brought me a great deal of pleasure and some important recognition.

I was asked to deliver the *Shabbat* morning sermon at the very first URJ Small Congregations Conference in Nashville on April 6, 1991. I based my sermon on a letter that was written in May 1926 and is part of my ex-wife's family history. The letter was written by a father to his son. I talked about the pride and the joy felt by a father and a son as a result of their involvement with the Jewish communities in the towns in which they lived. In preparing the sermon, I talked to several my congregation's past presidents and quickly understood that they did not share feelings of pride and joy about their involvement in the Jewish community. After explaining this in the sermon, I went on to say:

> They understood it as an obligation. They understood it as a responsibility. They understood it as the natural culmination of years of involvement in synagogue life. They didn't understand it as a source of joy and pride. They didn't understand it as an opportunity for personal fulfillment and personal growth. It was instead something that was necessary or inevitable or, "well, somebody had to do it." Being involved at

that level with the synagogue should be more than the inevitable, the duty, the responsibility, the obligation. The sense of *Koved*, the sense of honor, the sense of joy that once upon a time was part of our enterprise seems somehow to have been lost and gone. We need to rediscover it.

I continued along these lines for a moment or two and then came back to tie it in specifically with small congregations:

There are too many of us in the rabbinate and in the lay leadership who somehow or other seem to feel that if we are involved with a small congregation, there is something wrong. There are too many of my colleagues who see their careers the way I mapped mine out in 1959. A small congregation is something through which you pass on the way to greater glory and greater fulfillment. Lay leadership will ask rabbis, "Why do you want to have your contract renewed, why aren't you moving on to something better?" Which is euphemistic, of course, for something bigger. Obviously, we feel enough for this rabbi that we want him to be successful, we want her to move on to something better. Why can't we understand the possibility of success in a congregation that is relatively small?

I referred again to the father who wrote this wonderful letter to his son in 1926 and indicated that they had found personal success and personal pleasure in their Jewish lives in two very small congregations. I continued:

> They found success in their Jewish lives in those two communities and in those two synagogues. I suggest to you that we can, should, and will do the same.

Immediately following the service on *Shabbat* morning, Rabbi Alexander Schindler, then President of the URJ, approached me and put his arm around my shoulder. He wished me *Shabbat Shalom* and then said, "You are never going to speak at one of these conferences again." I asked him, "Why? Did I do something wrong?" "Yes, you did," he said. "You spoke better than I did last night." I assume he was kidding. Rabbi Kahan felt good enough about my sermon to ask me to transcribe it from the tape and send him a copy. He then mailed it to everyone who had attended that first URJ Small Congregations Conference.

A few months later, in agreement with the chairperson of the Small Congregations Committee named J. B. Tennenbaum, Rabbi Kahan asked me if I would be willing to represent the Small Congregations Department of the URJ on the Joint Commission on Jewish Education. Since religious education has always been a particular interest of mine, and since I felt that I might have something to contribute, I readily agreed. Unfortunately, neither the URJ nor my congregation had the sufficient funds to underwrite my expenses. Therefore, in the three or four years that I served, I could not attend all the meetings. The URJ made great efforts to include a wide range of individuals on its various committees and commissions. It was too bad that the Union couldn't find a way to provide travel and lodging expenses for those of us who cannot be funded from someone else's budget or from our own. It just doesn't seem proper to me that the only ones who managed to volunteer their time to the Union were folks with organizational support or deep pockets.

My relationship with the Small Congregations Department and the Joint Commission brought me another opportunity that I greatly appreciated. Rabbi Kahan called me on the phone from New York to ask if I would be willing to update a URJ manual on religious education in small congregations authored by Rebecca and Louis Lister in 1977. I agreed, with the stipulation that my daughter, Debi, coauthor the manual with me. URJ staff readily agreed. Debi is a 1980 graduate of HUC-JIR, Los Angeles, with a Master's Degree in Jewish Religion Education. She subsequently earned the designation RJE (Reform Jewish Educator) and was granted a Doctor of Jewish Religious Education from HUC.

As we began our work together, it became clear to both of us that updating the previous manual would not be adequate. With the permission of Rabbi Kahan and Seymour Rossel, then Director of the URJ Department of Education and the Commission on Reform Jewish Education, we planned a book. It was published by URJ Press in 1996 and titled, *A Guide To Small Congregation Religious Schools*. It has, so we are told, sold very well and has been featured in displays and at workshops at URJ Biennials, Regional Biennials, and the Small Congregations Conference.

The publication of that book was followed by a request from Robert E. Tornberg. He asked us to write a major chapter on *The Small Congregation* for a handbook that he was editing for Alternatives in Religious Education Publishing in Denver. *The Jewish Educational Leader's Handbook* was published in the summer of 1998.

Religious education has always been a primary interest of mine. When the opportunity presented itself, wrote two articles for *Compass*, the religious education magazine of the URJ. One dealt with adult education in a small isolated congregation and the other dealt with a model of a *tzedakah* program for religious schools. The Conference Journal, published by the CCAR, printed an article of mine dealing with some of the issues in religious education for *Bar/Bat mitzvah* and Confirmation.

Additionally, through my membership on the Outreach Committee of the Southeast Region of the URJ, I was invited to present a position paper at a workshop on the role of the non-Jew in the synagogue. That led to the same kind of assignment at a URJ Biennial. That, in turn, brought me a request from Dru Greenwood, Director of the Commission on Reform Jewish Outreach, to contribute an article in one of their manuals, *Defining The Role of The Non-Jew In The Synagogue: A Resource For Congregations*, which was published by the URJ in 1991. My article was entitled, *The Role of the Non-Jewish Parent in Synagogue Life Cycle Ceremonies, a Rabbi's Reflections*. That was so well received that the Commission asked me to write another article for a manual published two years later, *A Supplemental Process Guide For Congregations*. My article dealt with our experiences at Beth Israel Congregation in Florence, South Carolina and was called, *The Non-Jewish Spouse in the Synagogue-One Congregation's Process and Results*. The opportunity to write for publication brought me a great deal of recognition as well as a significant boost for my ego and my pride.

I have attended many services in black churches because I love the music and the preaching style of many black clergy. On one occasion, that experience made up for a significant mistake on my part. I traveled about 25 miles east of Florence, South Carolina, to Marion in order to conduct a funeral for a congregant and a friend, Dr. Ira Barth. He had lived in Marion for a very long time and had practiced there for approximately 35 years. He was the first doctor, and for a very long time the only doctor, that had a fully integrated waiting room. A patient was a patient, skin color made no difference. Therefore, when he died, most of those in attendance at the graveside funeral were black. About 250 people were there in total.

My son, Scott, had been home for a visit about two weeks earlier. At my request, he washed my car and cleaned it on the inside. What I didn't know was that he had gone so far as to clean the glove compartment. He took everything out and left all of it on a table in the garage. I wasn't aware of the fact that I was supposed to find the contents of my glove compartment, sort through it, throw some stuff away, and return the rest. So, when I arrived at the cemetery and opened the glove compartment in order to take out the *Rabbi's Manual* which I kept there, I found the glove compartment completely empty. The funeral was scheduled to begin in seven or eight minutes and I certainly had no opportunity for a 50-mile round trip.

I had done enough funerals so that it was possible to proceed without the manual, though it would have been a big help. The text of the 23rd Psalm was printed in the little program which the funeral director distributed to those who were present. That helped because it gave us something to do together. Don't ask what words I used, because I don't remember. Just know I started out and after a moment or two sounds came back to me from those who were present. Words like: "Tell it, brother," "Amen, Rabbi," and "Hallelujah, praise Jesus!" Before I realized what was happening, I slipped into the rhythm and the cadence of the typical black pastor that I had listened to on so many occasions. That style only seemed to fuel the response from the black people who were present and increased the extent and number of raised eyebrows on my own congregants.

Everything went very well until I searched in my mind for a particular word and lost the rhythm. I never got it back and so I asked everybody to join me in reciting the Psalm in a moment of silent prayer and then *Kaddish*. Ira's sons, both of whom were members of the synagogue, told me that it was the strangest and best Jewish funeral that they had ever attended. Independently they each told me that they were positive their dad would have loved it!

I arrived in South Carolina in July of 1984. I immediately became involved in the association of clergy and met Father John Coffey, priest of the local Roman Catholic parish. We became good friends because we discovered that we had many interests in common. In December, he came to my office at the synagogue to tell me that I was to be his roommate at a conference for clergy on substance abuse that was taking place that January in Charleston. He showed me the promotional materials and I agreed to go. I must admit that prior to my attendance I had very little knowledge of this problem and its effect on the religious community. The conference was held under the auspices of the Pastoral Care Committee (PCC) of the South Carolina Commission on Alcohol and Drug Abuse (SCCADA). It was the eighteenth or nineteenth such annual conference. I discovered later that it was the only one of its kind in the nation at the time.

The programming was excellent. The speakers were stimulating and the workshops proved to be very enlightening and useful. Unfortunately, the entire content of every aspect of the program was totally Christian in its emphasis and I felt somewhat out of place. Following the banquet on the last evening, I approached Jerry McCord, the Executive Director of SCCADA and shared with him my feelings of being left out. He informed me that he had been the director of the Commission since its inception 25 years earlier, he had personally formed the PCC, and that he had worked diligently to be inclusive in terms of clergy from all faith communities. He indicated that he had never been able to get a rabbi from South Carolina (Orthodox, Conservative, or Reform) to attend one of these Working Conferences. He was pleased that I had done so and asked if I would be willing to accept an appointment to be a member of the PCC. I enthusiastically agreed and I continued to serve until I left South Carolina during the summer of 1995. Sadly, even with personal letters and phone calls, I never got another Rabbi to attend, even those living in Charleston.

My ten years on this committee and my exposure to clergy from almost every religious faith represented in the state proved to be very important to me. I established many friendships, some of which continue. During the ten years that I was on the PCC, I served two years as its secretary, two years as its vice chairman (which made me the coordinator of the annual conference), and two years as the PCC chairman. During my last year, the commission was reorganized under a new governor into the South Carolina Department of Alcohol and Other Drug Abuse services. Jerry McCord, who had served brilliantly for almost 35 years, was retired so that the directorship could go to one of the new governor's strong supporters. The new director had absolutely no experience in any form of substance abuse work. She did not understand the need for substance abuse education, prevention, intervention, or aftercare. Within eighteen months after I left South Carolina, the PCC ceased to exist. Clergy no longer received the necessary training which I did during my ten-year affiliation with this wonderful governmental agency. It was a real pleasure to work with a true professional like Jerry McCord who was the pioneering leader of this kind of government involvement in substance abuse programs.

When I attended my last Working Conference in 1995, the PCC presented me with a plaque which prominently and proudly hung in my synagogue office. Its wording is as follows:

> The Pastoral Care Committee of the South Carolina Department of Alcohol and other Drug Abuse services expresses appreciation to Larry Mahrer for dedication, leadership and friendship. 1985–1995

Mike Bruce, pastor of the United Methodist Church in Quinby which was just outside of Florence, became one of my best friends. He has since moved to New Ellenton, South Carolina, then on to Charleston, and now back to a large church in Florence. We communicate regularly. At least once a year I spend four or five days with him and his family. Every time I visit, I'm asked to teach a class or speak in the church and I almost feel as if his Methodist church is a second religious home for me.

Another good friend is David Templeton, originally a Presbyterian minister and now with the United Church of Christ. He and Mike both became members of the PCC and both, eventually, served as its chairman. Unfortunately, it was on Mike's watch that PCC died. David was a clinical chaplain on the staff of a hospital in Greenville, South Carolina, that had both in and outpatient substance abuse programs. At the time of this writing, he was working in the same kind of situation in New England. I truly value my friendships with both pastors and cherish the times that we have spent together. I have learned a great deal from both and have come to a much greater understanding of the differences and the similarities of our various religious communities.

Another member of the Committee was David Coker, a Pentecostal Holiness pastor from Georgetown, South Carolina. He and I were two of six speakers at one of our Working Conference's major programs entitled, *Unity Within Diversity*. When it came his time to talk, he described for our audience the fact that his tradition prohibited the use of tobacco and alcohol in any of their various forms. He indicated that many of us on the PCC smoked and some drank socially. He told the group that I had approached him the first time that we all went out to dinner together, indicating that I would say something to everybody else if he wanted me to because I was aware of the position taken by his denomination. His response was to the effect that he didn't demand that others hold to his faith commitments unless they were members of his church, so we could go ahead and smoke if we wanted to. We could have a beer if that was our pleasure and all that he would do would be to fan any smoke away from his face if it came in that direction. When he mentioned this in his talk, he said that my approach to him truly opened his eyes to the potential for interreligious cooperation. He referred to me as his brother and walked over to where I was sitting to give me one of the nicest hugs I have ever had in my life. When he returned to the lectern, he indicated that he was inviting me to come to speak at his church some Sunday morning so that, possibly, his membership could have as positive an experience with a rabbi as he had done.

I did make that trip. He told me to arrive at about 10:30, which I did. As I walked toward the building, I could hear very loud jazz music and equally loud congregational singing. He met me in the hall and when I asked what was happening he said, "Oh, our service began at 9:00 and we'll be ready for you in a few minutes. I really didn't think that you needed to sit through the first hour and a half." We walked into the sanctuary and when the song was finished, he led the congregation in prayer, praising me and introducing me at the same time. He then welcomed me to his pulpit and told me that I could speak for up to 45 minutes. I thanked him and then began my remarks by telling his congregation that if I continued a sermon up to 20 minutes, people in my congregation began to look at their watches. At 25 minutes they began to point to their watches or to hold them up to their ears. I said that I would be very surprised if I talked that long that morning, and I didn't. It was a very interesting and exceedingly different environment in which to speak.

When I arrived at Temple Emanu-El in Dothan, I discovered an ongoing adult education program involving two or three people. To build on that success, I offered a course in the fall for the adults among our membership and another one in the spring. The attendance at each was in the range of four to five people. Because I successfully taught in other congregations as well as in a parochial high school and on college campuses, I searched for a way to make my teaching in Dothan more significant. With the approval of the Board of Trustees, I opened future adult education programs to the general community. I initially limited attendance to twenty or twenty-five and eventually opened it up to as many as thirty-five. Over the course of a few years I developed a list of more than eighty members of the general community, some coming from as far as forty miles away, who had participated in these adult education activities. In each case, the course was announced to our congregants first. Then, after about ten days, a mailing was sent to people who had studied with me previously and an announcement was made to the general public in the newspaper. As I said, members of the general community, representing a wide range of faith communities, participated enthusiastically and in large numbers. Unfortunately, I never had more than three or four of my own congregants register for any of these courses, and never more than two who stayed through the entire program.

One of the participants was the wife of the local Presbyterian pastor named Joe Johnson, who was mentioned previously in my discussion of the Dothan Ministerial Association and in the chapter on Social Action. Her participation led her husband to eventually talk to me about co-teaching some programs for our two congregations and for my already existing general community audience. Joe and I eventually taught ten such courses, the longest being one and a half hours per week for six consecutive weeks, with outstanding success. Success is measured both in terms of the number enrolled, the number who attend, and the level of spoken participation and feedback that we both receive. We had about 600 people who studied with us at least once.

I find the model of opening adult education programs to the general community to be a potential boon for small congregations that really cannot support a significant program with their own membership. In addition, it certainly is very worthwhile for the rabbi to teach the community on subjects of Jewish interests. Our local newspaper and one of our TV stations found this approach to adult education so sufficiently newsworthy that it was featured on a couple of occasions.

I know that I have said this before, but the myriad opportunities that I have had in my career to make friends with clergy from the Christian community have had a profound effect on my life. I have heard too many of my rabbinic colleagues say, "Why bother. It won't make any difference." In terms of anti-Semitism, Christian attitudes toward Jews, and teaching and preaching in the various churches, I think that friendship with a rabbi can make a great deal of difference. Furthermore, I think that my own rabbinate has been greatly improved as I have come to understand the many men and women who are my colleagues on the other side of the street. In our discussions I have had to sharpen my intellect. I have had to go back to my office to research the answers to their questions. Thus, they have forced me to raise the level of my study of my own tradition. Lastly, many of these people have been my friends for a long, long time.

Being a member of the clergy can be a very lonely profession. Frequently we can find nonthreatening colleagues and friends among the clergy from other religious traditions. They understand our loneliness. They understand some of our frustrations. They understand what we are going through because they experience similar things every day of their professional lives. They have been a blessing to me.

The Perfect Rabbi

At the time of this writing, I served eight congregations and obviously went through the interview process many more times. I always wondered exactly what it was that the members of a congregation search committee were looking for as they brought rabbis into their community for interviews.

Three years after accepting the rabbinate in a congregation which shall remain unnamed, I sat down to talk with the chairman of the committee that had selected me. I asked him, three years after the fact, what it was that he and his committee were seeking. He began by describing the relationship between congregation and rabbi as a marriage. He continued to describe how there must be give and take, compromise, and a sharing of a clear direction and goal. After a few more moments of reflection, he said something to the effect that his original statement sounded good, but it probably wasn't accurate. He knew that many of the members of his committee were looking for the perfect rabbi. He also understood, as some of his committee members did not, that such an individual did not exist. I told him that I agreed and suggested that most of the rabbis that I knew were excellent people and extremely competent professionals. Some of them had specific areas of interests in which they could be described as exceptional experts. I introduced him to the concept of *kol bo,* the rabbi who is a well prepared professional and who has some skills in every aspect of their profession. He suggested that the idea made sense. When I left that congregation, he would try to convince the committee searching for my replacement that they ought to keep the idea of *kol bo* in mind.

In Columbia, South Carolina, the newspaper is intended to serve the entire state and it is unsurprisingly called *The State.* On August 22, 1997, they printed a piece entitled, *Looking For The Perfect Rabbi,* by Stanley P. Riebam. I'm not at all certain how this clipping got into my file, neither do I have any idea who this gentleman is. In answer to the question what we want of our rabbis, Mr. Riebam wrote:

> If we were synagogue *machers* appointed to a search committee for a spiritual leader, and we set down an honest list of functions our rabbi must perform, the perfect candidate might well elude us. The Rabbi must be shepherd of the flock, leader in the community, emissary to the nations. He must be a scholar and teacher, orator and fundraiser, therapist and counselor. He must also be role

model and friend, and he must join in both our joy and our sorrows, presiding over each with wisdom and comfort as appropriate, mindful always of our dignity and his own, and the dignity of his office. It goes without saying that the perfect rabbi must also be a perfect politician and strictly adhere to the ritual requirements of the individual synagogue. Have I left anything out? Probably, but you get the point. We expect a great deal of our rabbis.

He goes on to say that he believes that we expect too much of our pulpit rabbis, because no individual can be all things to all people. Each has strengths and weaknesses. He talked about how as an adult he still goes to rabbis with his problems. Occasionally the problems are philosophical, intellectual, or matters of *Halachah*. But, most often, the problems are deeply personal and troubling. Usually, they are family matters and problems that arose in connection with the lifecycle events. He then goes on to say:

> It has always been the individual rabbi's response to what was important to me that defined that rabbi for me. The rabbi was a "good rabbi" if he showed compassion, humanity. The rabbi was a "bad rabbi" if he by word or deed or manner, dismissed me. If a "good rabbi" gave a bad sermon, I still thought the world of him. If the "bad rabbi" gave an eloquent sermon, I was not impressed.

I think that Mr. Riebam is highly accurate both in his description of the expectations of a rabbi as well as of his definitions of and reactions to the "good" or "bad" rabbi. He clearly has thought this through. It is a lesson that all of us, rabbis and lay people alike, must learn. Too often, we do not.

The Department of Adult Jewish growth of the URJ publishes a weekly interpretation of the *Sidra*. For the week of July 6-12, 1997, Rabbi Charles A. Kroloff, senior rabbi of Temple Emanu-El of Westfield, New Jersey, was the author. The title that he used was *What Is The Promised Land?* which is based on *Parashat Chukat*. In Numbers, Chapter 20, we read that God, "instructed Moses and his brother to take a rod, assemble the community, and ordered the rock to yield its water." Kroloff goes on to explain that instead of following instructions, Moses made three mistakes: he struck the rock, he called his people "rebels," and it did not include his brother, Aaron, as he had been told to do. Kroloff continues:

> We could stop right here, list Moses' many shortcomings (impatience, anger, self-centeredness, lack of faith), and conclude that he did fail to reach his goal. But that would be a mistake because the deeper truths in this story can help us in our own lives. While Moses was a great leader, he was an imperfect human being, like you and me. He made many of the same mistakes we make.
>
> But the truth is that he was not a failure, but a success. If we measure success by whether we leave

the world better than we found it, he scored extremely high. If we measure success by how much we have done to strengthen the Jewish people, he was a success without a peer.

Moses really did reach the Promised Land. Perhaps he did not actually enter Canaan, but he brought his people right to the edge, and despite his shortcomings, he led a remarkable life.

So it is with us. Even if we experience personal loss or disappointment, if we live ethical lives, if we spend enough time with those we love, if we direct our talents and resources to those who need us, if we sanctify our days with Jewish tradition, we, too, can say that we have arrived at our Promised Land.

I think that Kroloff's very brief analysis is brilliant. I read it at a time when my own life was suffering the consequence of a tragic error that I made. It certainly helped me come to terms with myself and with my rabbinate.

But, more importantly to me, he said something that I have always taught but can't remember reading anywhere. When Kroloff states that Moses was human, he emphasizes why I have a continuous love affair with the Hebrew Bible. All the individuals who populate its pages are completely human. Each one has moments of joy and times of sadness. Most of them do wonderful things, as well as things that we would choose not to repeat in our own lives. If the characters in the bible were not human, we would quickly conclude that they could not serve as role models for us. If their problems and their behavior were not somewhat like ours, we would never be able to learn anything from them. If this were the situation, then the Bible and the rabbinical literature that grew out of it would be irrelevant for us as people. Thankfully, that isn't the case.

I was with a congregant many years ago who was quite despondent over having made a very poor choice in terms of his personal behavior. He thought that he would never be able to live it down or overcome the negative feelings that some people had about him. I reminded him of some of the stories that he and I had studied together in a bible class. I asked if he remembered the story of Abraham chasing his first son out of the household. I asked if he remembered Abraham passing Sarah off as his sister to protect himself. I asked him if he remembered that David committed adultery and also entered into a conspiracy to murder his lady friend's husband. Of course, he remembered those instances, and even suggested a few that I hadn't brought up. I then asked him if he admired David and Abraham. When he indicated that he did, I asked him why. His reply was that they rose above those problems, worked them out, and that in total their lives were beneficial and good. I then asked him to evaluate his own life, and for the first time in many weeks I saw him smile as he understood my point. The humanity of the Hebrew Bible is, in my opinion, its greatest asset. As Rabbi Kroloff pointed out, we are not perfect, we are human. We should revel in our humanness because that is what permits us to be real people.

Several years ago, I made a tragic mistake which caused a great deal of pain to people that I loved and cared about, and to the congregation which I was serving. After a couple of months, I entered into a counseling relationship with a local Lutheran pastor who was also a certified clinical counselor. She led me through hours of discussion very similar to the things that I have written in the previous paragraph. I came to realize that I had understood those concepts intellectually, while never internalizing them emotionally. I eventually improved and began to feel a little bit better about myself with her help and the hours of conversation that I spent with my friend Mike Bruce while visiting in his home. Nonetheless, I wasn't healed even though I thought that I probably was.

I attempted to talk to or write to many of the people who had been most affected by my behavior. Some I reached, some refused to take telephone calls from me, while some chose not to answer my letters. But I did make the effort and felt better for it. *T'Shuvah* works!

What really made a difference was reading Chuck Kroloff's one-page article in July of 1997. Maybe it was seeing those familiar ideas expressed by a colleague. Maybe it was the fact that they came across my desk at exactly the right time. Whatever it was, he lifted my spirits tremendously and I became the smiling, happy man that I once was. My friends and my children noticed the difference and commented on it. Their validation of my therapy was also a great help. It marked the beginning of my recovery.

As part of this recovery process, the CCAR required me to meet with a rabbinic mentor. I was very fortunate that they selected my good friend, Rabbi David Baylinson of Montgomery. We began to meet for lunch on a regular basis in a small town halfway between Montgomery and Dothan. If I remember correctly those luncheons began in 1996.

Along these same lines, this section was written two days before I left for the west coast to attend my first meeting of the National Association of Retired Reform Rabbis (NAORRR). Though I was not retired at the time, I was able to be a part of this group because I met the age requirement, something like AARP. I was certain that I knew most of the members of NAORRR because we were at HUC together, we attended CCAR conventions together years ago, we worked at URJ camps together, and these are the men that I consider to be my true colleagues.

My troubles aren't over. I still have a long way to go. But I am now confident that everything will be resolved in a very positive way. I am feeling better about myself and about my rabbinate. I am once again enjoying support from my friends and some of my colleagues. I had not permitted myself that pleasure before because I didn't think I deserved it. Kroloff spoke to me because, except for this one incident, I have led a worthwhile life and have had a successful career. May both continue.

"I Always Knew You Weren't Really God"

She was about two and a half years old and the younger child in a family that was quite active in our congregation. Her older brother was nine or ten. Her mother had been married previously, and the older child was from her first marriage. Both mother and son converted to Judaism before the daughter was born.

She came to the synagogue building one day with her parents, walked up to me, and said, "Hello God!" I was surprised and her parents were embarrassed. This behavior continued for over a year. Whenever she saw me, she referred to me as God. At first, neither her parents nor I could understand what was happening and when they asked her, she had no answer.

Eventually, when her parents were about to leave the house one evening to come to the synagogue for a program, she asked where they were going, and her father responded by saying, "We are going to the synagogue." When she asked why, his reply was, "Because that's where God is." No sooner had he said that phrase than he began to understand his daughter. He realized that he said something like it almost every time they came to the synagogue building. Of course, every time she came to the building, I was the one person who was always there. The association was quickly made. I was God, at least in her mind and out of her mouth, for a little more than a year.

At noon one Sunday, she and her parents had come to pick up her brother after Religious School. As she walked out of the Social Hall door (where I always stood to say goodbye to everybody) and toward the parking lot, she flipped me a little salute and said, "So long, Larry." Her mother, who at one time had been a Southern Baptist, almost fainted at that level of familiarity. Though I requested that adults call me either Rabbi Larry or Larry, she always referred to me simply as Rabbi. Here was her young daughter calling me by my first name. The kid walked out the door with her mother, down about three steps to the sidewalk, then turned around and came back in the building by herself. She looked me right straight in the eye and said, "I always knew you weren't really God." Then she left. Thereafter, until I left that congregation, I was Rabbi Larry. Her parents recovered from the shock and her brother told and retold that story until everyone in the congregation had heard it seven or eight times.

As I began working on this book, going back through my files, and looking at old synagogue bulletins, I recalled my experience on Broad Street in Columbus with Rabbi Jerome Folkman. I wrote about it at the very beginning of the first chapter. At the time that this little girl began to call me God, and then eventually told me that she knew that I wasn't God, I never connected it with the story from Columbus, Ohio. But there clearly is a relationship.

In both instances, two young children who were approximately the same age tended to associate God exclusively with the synagogue, the rabbi with the synagogue, and the rabbi with God. Obviously at that age, at least for those two children, nobody had helped to associate God with all people, all human life, and all places.

There are, however, a multitude of excellent storybooks and texts for very young children to assist them in understanding that God is everywhere that we, as people, might want God to be. My experience as an educator tells me that this is a lesson that even the youngest children can learn. Maybe we need to listen carefully to these two kids, remember their stories which occurred about 35 years apart, and begin to talk to our children at a much younger age about the part that God plays in our lives. On their own level, they certainly are willing to understand and use the term.

The End of the Line

I wrote this final chapter in February 2006. At that time, I was the part time Rabbi of Temple Emanu-El in Dothan, Alabama. By the end of June 2006, my agreement with that congregation came to an end and I moved on. That might have sounded strange for someone who was going to be 74 years old by that date. With all its ups and downs, I enjoyed my rabbinic career and I simply did not want it to conclude abruptly.

I hoped that I would be able to find another small congregation which was looking for a rabbi to live in the area and conduct services for the holidays, one or two Sabbaths per month, and the necessary lifecycle events. I wanted to slow down, but not disengage myself from the rabbinate or from Jews and Judaism. Chronologically, I may have been old. But I did not feel that way. I was in good health. I managed my present assignments very well. I was quite active in the general community with many hours of volunteer time. I went to the gym regularly, with no real complaints. So, why quit totally?

More importantly, I discovered through my very enjoyable participation in the National Association of Retired Reform Rabbis and my attendance at their annual January conventions, that I could still do 'it'. Whatever 'it' might be. Seriously, I have learned that many of us at my age, and significantly older, can continue to make contributions to the Jewish community, the synagogue, and to the lives of individual Jews and their families.

Those of you who are not rabbis might have some difficulty in understanding how important the concept of contributing is in reality. I did not have this feeling at the beginning of my career, but I do now. It has grown steadily over time, until it has become the major motivating factor in all that I do professionally. When I stood on the *bimah* at an *Erev Shabbat* service and put my hands on the shoulders of the 13-year-old who had just completed her *Bat mitzvah*, I knew that I have had an impact on her life and on her family. You have no idea how much that pleased and satisfied me.

I also discovered that my satisfaction is not an ego issue. It used to be but is no longer. I learned to see beyond myself into the lives of the children and adults with whom I work. I came to realize that they matter. I do not. That separation of ego from professionalism was a remarkable moment in my life. It did not come easily, but it did arrive. I still wonder if I consciously worked at it, or if it occurred on its own. I am not certain that I know the answer, nor am I sure that it matters.

I discussed this with some of my colleagues at NAORRR, both older and younger. They tended to agree with what I wrote in the last few paragraphs. They came to the same enlightenment and most of them weren't exactly positive about how and when the change in their personalities manifested itself. They are universally happy that it did, however.

I guess what I am trying to say is that over a career which has spanned 47 years so far, I have become a much better person and rabbi. I am eternally grateful for that happenstance. I only wish that there was some way to guide others to the understanding which I have reached. I doubt that it can be accomplished. I think it is too personal to be taught or learned, except by experience.

I will conclude by listing the congregations I have served over the years. Each has had an impact on who I became. I feel that I have made contributions to the lives of the synagogues and to their members and to the communities in which I lived and worked.

Temple Beth El	Battle Creek, MI	1959–1962
Beth Hillel Temple	Kenosha, WI	1962–1966
Anshai Emeth	Peoria, IL	1966–1972
B'nai El	St. Louis, MO	1972–1973
Mount Sinai Congregation	Wausau, WI	1977–1982
Temple Beth Shalom	Topeka, KS	1982–1984
Beth Israel Congregation	Florence, SC	1984–1995
Temple Emanu-El	Dothan, AL	1995–2006

If you have sharp eyes, you will have noted a gap in that sequence of years. I left B'nai El under unhappy circumstances but stayed in the community for another year and a half. I occupied my time by enrolling in the University of Missouri - St. Louis and earned a Master's of Education degree, with major emphasis in secondary education. Following that, I worked at *Hamakor Judaica* in Chicago. I served as their educational consultant and staffed the retail store. At the same time, I visited Congregation B'nai Israel in Oshkosh, Wisconsin, two weekends a month and taught Confirmation Classes and adult education for several Chicago Reform congregations. When I returned to the pulpit rabbinate, in Wausau, it followed a clear decision to dedicate the remainder of my professional career to small congregations only. That was a wise choice and it has served me well.

As stated earlier, it has been a busy and full career. I am pleased that I have been able to share some of it with you. I hope that you got as much out of the reading as I did out of the remembering and the writing.

May we all be blessed for the rest of our lives as we have been in the past. *Ken Y'hi Ratzon!*

Epilogue
"I just can't remember!"

I thought I had finished this book. Then something happened that I wanted to describe.

In the fall of 1997, I got a phone call from a young woman that I hadn't spoken with since she was a teenager in the early 1970s. She told me that the spring of 1998 was the 25th anniversary of her Confirmation and that she was planning a reunion. Since I was the rabbi who officiated at that *Erev Shavuot* service, I was expected to attend and the final choice of a date would be dependent upon my calendar. We looked at my schedule and I gave her a few alternatives. She said that she would check around with the other members of the class and be back in touch within a few days. It was at that point that she reminded me that my son, Jeff, was a member of that class and that the two of them used to date occasionally.

The result of all this planning was a reunion of the 1973 Confirmation Class of B'nai El Congregation in St. Louis over a weekend in June 1998. The incumbent Rabbi and the board of the congregation agreed to cooperate with the previous students, and we arranged to conduct services on *Erev Shabbat* using the creative liturgy which the class had prepared for their Confirmation in 1973. Its theme was, not surprisingly, peace. Since Confirmation was on *Shavuot*, the liturgy made specific references to the holiday which we decided to continue to include. We only made a few adaptations, which were adding in *Shabbat* candle lighting (*Kiddush*), using the congregation's present way of introducing *Kaddish*, and reading the list of names for *Yahrzeit*.

My long-ago students and I gathered in a classroom about an hour before services were scheduled to begin. We divided the service among ourselves and proceeded into the Sanctuary. The class members arranged a truly beautiful *Oneg Shabbat*. About 150 people were at the service. Some of them were long time members of the congregation who came by to say hello to me. Others were regular *Erev Shabbat* attendees who had no specific attachment to this Confirmation reunion. The rest were the Confirmands' parents, some of their spouses, children, and friends that just tagged along.

On Saturday evening we gathered at a very nice private club for a dinner in one of their small dining rooms. One of the things that we did was simply go around the table and talk about what our lives had been like in the intervening 25 years and what we remembered of our time in Religious School, particularly in the Confirmation Class which I taught. Throughout all of this, one young woman kept saying, "I can't remember," or "Did we really do that?" After listening to her say that frequently on Friday night, and even more often on Saturday night, somebody finally asked her why she couldn't remember anything that happened when they were in the tenth grade. Her reply was that she and one of the other students in the Confirmation class would go to the parking lot, sit in one of the cars, and simply get stoned to the point where they were pretty much out of touch with whatever happened inside the building. They went through the motions. She attended class but was not present.

That certainly came as a surprise to me and to most of her classmates. I guess none of us were as observant or as discerning as we could have been or thought we were.

But the 25th anniversary reunion of a Confirmation is a wonderful idea! I would encourage others to do the same.

It has been a wonderful journey. It has been pleasurable and instructive to think back about my life and my career as a rabbi. I have derived a great deal of joy from the preparation of this manuscript. I pray that your reading it will bring you a measure of pleasure as well.

Rabbi Larry Mahrer

Afterword

My father stopped working on his manuscript in 2006. It was not ready to be published, as there remained many handwritten notes and edits throughout. There was plenty of proofreading and further editing that was necessary as well. A huge *thank you* to Rabbi Ron Klotz, Debi Rowe, Nilda Mahrer and Michelle Keck for assistance with the proofreading. Five pairs of eyes are indeed much better than one.

After he finished his assignment in Dothan, Alabama, it was on to Parrish, Florida for my father. He remained there for twelve years. For most of his time in Florida, he taught adult education classes at a nearby synagogue. He also had a student with whom he worked with directly for about 10 years.

During his later years in Florida, he was diagnosed with Memory Impairment, and more recently with Alzheimer's

Disease. This has largely affected his short-term memory. He still revels in telling stories from his past. Recently, as of this writing, he moved into a Jewish assisted living facility near my wife, Nilda, and me in southern New Jersey. He is very happy there and has acclimated well to the change. While the facility is Jewish and keeps Kosher, about 20 percent of the residents are not Jewish. My father has remarked several times that he enjoys the interesting challenge of discovering who is and who is not Jewish.

Working on this book has been quite a remarkable project. While I knew the majority of the events related within, it did give me much insight into why I often felt that others "borrowed my father" when I was young. The perspective of the child knew simply that Dad was not at home like other dads. As an adult, I can see that he was doing important work, and can fully appreciate his time spent away.

Scott Mahrer – June 2019

Glossary

in order of appearance

Shabbat Sabbath (Introduction)

Oneg Shabbat "Joy of the Sabbath", a social gathering held after Sabbath services, usually including food. (Introduction)

bimah a raised platform or altar in a synagogue (Introduction)

Torah first five books of the Hebrew Bible (Introduction)

mezuzah a small box that is placed on the right doorpost of Jewish homes. Inside the box is a parchment scroll with verses from the Bible inscribed on it, including the *Sh'ma* prayer. (p. 2)

Erev the day/evening before (p. 3)

Pi'el a Hebrew root formation in Biblical Hebrew (p. 4)

Rosh HaShanah "Head of the Year", the Jewish New Year (p. 6)

shofar-an instrument made from a ram's horn/the horn of a ram (p. 7)

Sefer Torah the handwritten parchment scroll of the "Five Books of Moses", the holiest book in Judaism (p. 8)

Aliyot the honor (plural) of being called to read from the Torah (p. 9)

Sh'ma considered to be the most essential prayer in all of Judaism, an affirmation of God's singularity (p. 9)

Yom Kippur the Day of Atonement, is the holiest day of the year in Judaism (p. 10)

Kiddush blessing recited over wine to sanctify the Sabbath and Jewish holidays (p. 12)

Havdalah "separation", a Jewish religious ceremony that marks the symbolic end of the Sabbath and ushers in the new week (p. 29)

Shevah B'rachot "the seven blessings", traditional recited or chanted during a wedding ceremony (p. 33)

Yahrzeit "time of [one] year", anniversary of the day of the death of a relative (p. 47)

Yizkor a memorial service held by Jews on certain holy days for deceased relatives (p. 48)

Kaddish prayer traditionally recited in memory of the dead, although it makes no mention of death (p. 48)

Haftarah a portion from the Prophets read after the reading from the Torah on the Sabbath and festivals (p. 48)

Mitzvah "commandment", good deed (p. 49)

Menschlichkeit humanity (p. 49)

Aliyah the honor of being called upon to recite a blessing before and after the reading of the *Torah* (p. 49)

Maftir Yonah with its emphasis on the theme of repentance, the Book of Jonah has become a traditional part of the synagogue service on Yom Kippur (p. 49)

B'nai Mitzvah plural of *Bar Mitzvah*, "Son of the Commandment" (p. 51)

Va'anachnu a verse of the *Aleinu*, the closing prayer of a service (p.54)

Tikkun Olam "repair the world", an aspiration to behave and act constructively and beneficially (p. 73)

Midrash an ancient commentary on part of the Hebrew scriptures (p. 76)

Midrashim plural of *Midrash* (p. 76)

Shrie Gevalt to cry out (p. 78)

Halachah Jewish religious laws (p. 87)

Shabbat Shuvah "Sabbath [of] Repentance", the Shabbat that occurs during the Ten Days of Repentance between Rosh Hashanah, and Yom Kippur (p. 91)

Aleinu "It is our duty to praise", closing prayer of a service (p. 99)

Kol Nidre an Aramaic declaration recited in the synagogue at the beginning of the evening service on every Yom Kippur (p. 117)

Sh'ma Yisrael "Hear O Israel" [or "Listen, Israel"], the first words of the *Sh'ma*, considered to be the most essential prayer in all of Judaism, an affirmation of God's singularity (p. 120)

Yichus Yiddish word for "family tree" or genealogy, bragging rights based on respected family history, or "the chain of origin for a statement, creative work or object" (p. 130)

Sukkot festival named for the huts in which Jews are supposed to dwell during this week-long celebration. These flimsy *sukkot* represent the huts in which the Israelites dwelt during their 40 years of wandering in the desert after escaping from slavery in Egypt. (p. 130)

Chassid a member of a strictly orthodox Jewish sect, noticeable by their unique attire (fur hats [and/or black top hats/fedoras] and long coats) (p. 165)

Amidah "standing", refers to a series of blessings recited while standing that is the core of every Jewish worship service (p. 165)

Chuppah a canopy beneath which Jewish marriage ceremonies are performed (p. 173)

Shoah Holocaust (p. 175)

Ner Tamid "eternal flame", a light that hangs in front of and above the ark in the synagogue that is a symbol of God's eternal presence (p. 178)

Menorot plural of *menorah* "lamp", refers to either the seven-branched candelabra found in a synagogue or the nine-branched candelabra that is lit on the eight nights of Chanukah (p. 178)

Shabbat Shalom "Sabbath of peace", a common Sabbath greeting, used especially at the end of a Shabbat service (p. 185)

Machers important people, sometimes in the negative sense of self-importance; a bigwig (p. 199)

Sidra "order", "arrangement", weekly readings from the Five Books of Moses/*Torah* as part of the Sabbath service (p. 201)

Parashat Chukat Numbers 19:1–22:1 (p. 201)

Shavuot "weeks", festival that commemorates the anniversary of the day God gave the Torah to the entire Israelite nation assembled at Mount Sinai (p. 213)

Made in the USA
Columbia, SC
14 June 2020